JOURNAL OF INTEGRATIVE HUMANISM
GHANA
(INTEGRATING PERSPECTIVES)
VOLUME FOUR; NUMBER ONE
OCTOBER, 2014

First Published May, 2011

ISSN: 2026 - 6286

Website: www.intehumanismjournal.com

LIST OF CONTRIBUTORS

1. OGBONNAYA, LUCKY UCHENNA – Essien Ukpabio Presbyterian Theological College, Itu

2. PROF. G.O. OZUMBA – Department of Philosophy, University of Calabar, Calabar

3. V. C. A NWEKE – Department of Philosophy, University of Calabar, Calabar

4. LILY N. OZUMBA – Department of Political Science, University of Calabar, Calabar

5. ADIE EDWARD UGBADA – Department of Theatre and Media Studies, University of Calabar, Calabar

6. LILIAN ANWULIKA OKORO – Department of Theatre and Media Studies, University of Calabar, Calabar

7. ORIM, EUGENIA GABRIEL – Department of Theatre and Media Studies, University of Calabar, Calabar

8. LAWRENCE EKWOK – Department of Theatre and Media Studies, University of Calabar, Calabar

9. APEH, COLUMBA – Department of Theatre and Media Studies, University of Calabar, Calabar

10. SAMUEL ASUQUO EKANEM Ph.D – Department of Educational Foundation and Administration, Cross River University of Technology

11. FRANCIS FELIX EDET Ph.D – Department of Religious and Cultural Studies, University of Calabar

12. IWUCHUKWU, GODWIN CHINAEDU S. PhD – Department of Linguistics and Communication Studies, University of Calabar, Calabar

13. AFO DONALDSON USHIE – Department of Theatre and Media Studies, University of Calabar, Calabar

14. NDIMELE, ROSELINE IHUOMA PhD – Department of Linguistics and Communication/Igbo, Abia State University, Uturu.

15. NWOSU, ANN FRANCIS – Department of Political Science, University of Calabar, Calabar

16. NWOSU, FRANCIS MADUWUBA – Institute of Oceanography, University of Calabar, Calabar.

CONTENTS

1. A Critique of Ozumba's Spiritocentric Metaphysics
    - Ogbonnaya, Lucky Uchenna

2. Integrative Humanism and the Metaphysics of Spiritocentricism
    - Prof. G.O. Ozumba

3. From African Logic to the Development of Traditions of
    Logic in African Philosophy: An Integrativist Perspective
    - V. C. A. Nweke

4. Developing Rural Education in Nigeria
    - Lily N. Ozumba

5. Exploring the Potentials of Community Theatre as a Tool for
    Social Change: The Participatory Communication Method
    - Adie, Okoro, and Urim

6. Development of Nigerian Advertising and Media Exchange: A
    Post Modern Perspective
    - Apeh and Ekwok

7. Terrorism and Education: The Need for a Philosophy of
    Education In Nigeria
    - Samuel AsuquoEkanem, Ph.D

8. Boko Haram: A Legal and Biblical Perspective
    - Francis Felix Edet – Ph.D

9. The Role of Language in the Acquisition of Education and
    Technology: A Case Study of Igbo
    - Iwuchukwu, Chinaedu Ph.D

10. Proverbs as Evidence of Social Inequality in Igbo
    - Iwuchukwu Ph.D and Ndimele Ph.D

11. Understanding Empowerment for Sustainable Development in
    Nigeria: A Theatre and Participatory Communication Approach
    - Ugbada and Ushie

12.   Anaximander's Conception of the Urstoff and the Idea of Nke-
        Mbu in Integrative Humanism
        - Ogbonnaya, Lucky Uchenna

13.   Response to Climate Change for Sustainable Development: A
        Human Resource Development Approach.
        - Nwosu, A. F. & Nwosu, F. M.

A CRITIQUE OF OZUMBA'S SPIRITOCENTRIC METAPHYSICS
BY

OGBONNAYA, LUCKY UCHENNA
ESSIEN UKPABIO PRESBYTERIAN THEOLOGICAL COLLEGE
ITU
revluckyuogb@gmail.com

ABSTRACT
This work is of the view that Ozumba posits a metaphysics that bifurcates and polarizes reality. This is found in his 'spiritocentric metaphysics'. The metaphysics asserts that reality is more spiritual than physical since all reality moves towards becoming spiritual in the uwa mgbe ebi-ebi, where it will be united with the Nke-Mbu, which is spiritual. This work, therefore, posits that this view of Ozumba needs to be revisited and addressed based on the fact that it contradicts the Bible, which it claims to be its basic background, as well as African ontology that harmonizes contraries. It is only at this point that one can say that being or reality consists of spirit and matter. This work arrives at this conclusion using the methods of textual analysis, speculation, critique and synthesis.

Key-Words: *Humanocentric   Metaphysics,   Integrative   Humanism,
Integrativism, Nke-Mbu, Spiritocentric Metaphysics*

Introduction

Godfrey Okechukwu Ozumba is a Professor of philosophy in the department of philosophy, University of Calabar. He has developed a philosophical system or school of thought known as "Integrative Humanism". This philosophical system is one of the contemporary philosophical trends in Africa that is making great waves within, and outside Nigeria. This is because of its peculiar method and philosophy. It is a philosophy and method that does not look down on other existing philosophical methods or systems. It is a philosophy that sees other philosophies as important as itself and therefore incorporates them in the course of studying any reality. The philosophy also goes beyond doing philosophy from an empirical level to the spiritual level. This is to say that Ozumba adds a spiritual dimension to the already existing empirical way of doing philosophy or studying reality.

It is on this spiritual dimension of his philosophy that the present writer who is one of his students tends to look into, in order to bring out its implication to the branch of philosophy called metaphysics. Here, the writer

1

seeks to point to the originator of this philosophical system and other integrative humanists or integrativists (which the researcher is now part of) that the spiritocentric aspect of the philosophy of integrative humanism leads to what the present researcher terms "spiritocentric metaphysics", which is a bifurcating metaphysics. The work therefore calls for a reconsideration of this metaphysics. The aim for this reconsideration is to be able to provide answers to persons who may ask if this philosophy has fulfilled its objective of giving us "a broader and more comprehensive vision of reality" (Ozumba and Chimakonam 31), by proposing spiritocentric metaphysics.

An Overview on Integrative Humanism

There has been a call for a new way of doing philosophy in Africa and among African scholars, especially those within the field of philosophy. Integrative humanism or "Njikoka Amaka" is a product of such cry. It is a philosophical system that strives to go beyond every kind of philosophy that is strictly empirically based. It is in this light that Ozumba notes that:

> Integrative humanism is simply defined as a ratio-spiritocentric approach in understanding human existence, interpreting human affairs, and a rigorous philosophical attitude which takes into consideration, the spiritual and mundane dimensions of human existence and reality. It attempts philosophizing from the point of view of holistic truth bearing in mind that man is both mortal and/ immortal, spirit and body. Integrative humanism is both a philosophy and a method. (Philosophy and Method of 22; Integrative Humanism: The Spirit of 57)

Integrative humanism is a philosophical attitude towards life - human life and the entirety of reality. It studies all facets of reality as it affects humans directly or indirectly. According to Ozumba:

> This attitude takes a serious view that all parts of reality constituting matter and spirit, the plant and animal world as an integrated ecosystem of which no part can be isolated without dire consequences. Integrative humanism as a philosophy can therefore be applied as a beneficial approach in studying any facet of existent reality. (Ozumba, Philosophy and Method 23)

This philosophy in a way does not despise any existent reality or aspect of reality. All aspects of reality are considered to be important since they are brought "into harmonious whole" (Ozumba, "National Conscience..." 152).

The main concern of integrative humanism is how to gain knowledge or insight on existence in the cosmos, whether temporal or eternal existence. It is on this note that Ozumba asserts that:

> Our concerns have been how to know reality, deep things about life, about earthly existence, eternal existence and our relationship to other existent things and our environment and planets... Integrative humanism is therefore, the outcome of a deep, reflective brooding on the above questions and issues. Integrative humanism happens to be my own way of making meaning out the morass of intricate and *criss-crossing* mass of amorphous reality with which we have to deal as philosophers. (Integrative Humanism and Complementary Reflection 154)

The aim of integrative humanism is to give a more incisive and insightful view about reality. This is captured in the words of Ozumba thus: "integrative humanism does not deny the possibility of other equally consistent and coherent views about reality but indeed belies this aim of achieving higher, deeper, more profound and more comprehensive picture of reality" (Integrative Humanism and Complementary Reflection 154). With this way of discussing reality beyond a one-sided understanding, especially in positing that reality only consist of things within the physical world, without taking into cognizance its spiritual dimension; Integrative humanism notes that "philosophy is a systematic inquiry into the horizon of reality with the view to fathoming its many sided dimensions" (Integrative Humanism and Complementary Reflection 153).

Integrative humanism strives to give a more comprehensive understanding of reality by employing its method called 'integrativism'. This method of philosophizing is a polymethodic approach to reality. In other words, it is a multi-dimensional method used in approaching reality. It employs more than one method in inquiring about reality. This implies that integrative humanism does not use only one method but more than one possible method that leads to an insightful understanding of reality. It is in line with this that Ozumba writes that:

> Every ladder and equipment that will aid us to climb out of ignorance or what Asouzu calls the "the phenomenon of concealment" and which the Holy Writ aptly captures when

it says "my people are destroyed because of lack of knowledge" should be fully utilized. (Integrative Humanism and Complementary Reflection 154)

This does not imply that all methods go just as Paul Feyerabend's "everything goes" (348). Integrativism as a method of philosophy employs only methods or theories that are relevant for the particular study but does not discard the un-useful ones because they could be useful in another study.

Thus, integrativism is a method of synthesis. It synthesizes existent methods or approaches as well as theories of studying reality. It is also open to future philosophical methods that may be postulated since philosophy seeks to explain reality, which is still unfolding itself. Hence, it does not see any philosophical method or system as superior or more important than others. Instead of disregarding any method or theory, it integrates them based on their usefulness in order to arrive at a better understanding of reality. And when they are not useful they are not discarded, rather they are kept and used where and when they are needed. It does not see philosophical methods, systems or theories as complete in themselves or competing rivals but as what should be integrated to have a clearer picture of reality. Ozumba substantiates this thus:

> We have integrativism which is the method which seeks to penetrate our research with the potentials of exploring and harnessing the benefits of opposites, complementable units, theories and methods all with the view of vouchsafing a broader, more comprehensive understanding of reality. (A Rejoinder 26)

It is in this light that Chimakonam, Asuo and Agu aver that:

> This method demands that a researcher understands the kernel of different methods, the weaknesses and strengths of these methods, so that he can weld together their strengths in studying a given reality. This implies that he must first of all seek to understand the subject matter of his study by finding out its physical and transcendental aspects, so that the approach will be broad based and not one-sided or rift with bias and narrow-mindedness. (54)

It is based on this fact that it can be said that integrativism involves "synthetic, analytic, eclectic, syncretic, complementary and 'agglutinistic' tendencies" (*Philosophy and Method of* 38). It is a fusion of methods which involves sifting and gluing of necessary and useful methods in studying a given reality that has bearing with human well-being.

4

Spiritocentric Metaphysics in Ozumba's Integrative Humanism

Ozumba's integrative humanism hinges its concept of reality on the African conception of reality as he notes that "the primordial perception of reality by the African is derived from the ontological constitution of all things in an integrated mesh of mundanity and spirituality" (Integrative Humanism and Complementary Reflection 157). That is to say, for Ozumba, spirituality and mundanity are closely linked and intertwined such that it can be said that they always co-exist. Relating this to humankind, he notes that integrative humanism "seeks earthly and eternal good and is concerned with aggregating the best in being in order to ensure man's earthly and eternal bliss" (Integrative Humanism and Complementary Philosophy 159). By this, Ozumba is saying that "the undergirding objective of integrative humanism is the need to place man's physical and spiritual well-being at the centre of every intellectual endeavour" (Philosophy and Method of 19). This insight of the well-being of human being which is based on Ozumba's belief that the human being consists of physical and spiritual aspects has its root in his conception of reality, which Mesembe Ita Edet captures thus:

> This is because, it is clear that "integrative humanism" as Ozumba conceptualizes it advocates the integration of insights from the physical and spiritual dimensions of reality in tackling all human-based problems and quests for knowledge. This is clear and understood. (17)

This connotes that reality consists of two dimensions-the physical and spiritual dimensions. These two dimensions, according to Ozumba, are very important and indispensable in philosophizing and seeking to solve human problems. By extension the human being "has physical and transcendental sides" (Okeke and Agu 19). "Here, integrative humanism aims at a harmonious monistic concept of the human person" (Mamadu 47), as it posits according to Okeke, Asuo and Agu that "man as an entity... is composed of both physical and spiritual aspects" (53).

In spite of Ozumba's positing that the human being consists of physical and spiritual aspects, he goes on to assert that the spiritual aspect of the human being is superior to the physical aspect. This can be clearly inferred from his assertion that "man is a being unto eternity" (Ozumba, Philosophy and Method of 24). The question here is: if the human being is a being that continues to exist unto eternity, what aspect of human continues to exist in

5

eternity? Is it the entire human being? Or is it an aspect of human nature? Ozumba is of the view that the two constituent natures of human being do not exist to eternity. He holds that it is only the spiritual aspect of the human being that continues to exist unto eternity. This could be the rationale behind his terming his philosophy "spiritocentric humanism". Jonathan Okeke Chimakonam captures this better as he posits that:

> The concept (spiritocentric humanism) is a useful emphasis that demonstrates the primacy of spirit in our brand of humanism. Man for us has two aspects, the physical and the spiritual, with the latter being primary. In other words, our philosophy of integrative humanism is not just about harmonizing the physical and the spirit, it emphasizes the primacy of the spiritual over the physical hence, for example, we say that man is a being unto eternity. (Integrative Humanism: Extensions and Clarifications 78)

In a nutshell, Ozumba holds that man is proceeding from physical existence to spiritual existence. What is moving from the physical existence to the spiritual existence is nothing but the spiritual aspect of human being. It is this view that can be termed "spiritocentirc metaphysics".

The above view is said to be spiritocentric metaphysics because it is concerned with the spiritual well-being of human being than the physical. And in Ozumba's idea of human being as a being unto eternity, he sees the human spirit as what continues to exist. The implication of this is that in being and reality it is the spiritual that is eternal and superior. According to Chimakonam:

> Reality, being, man, life, purpose, etc., linger into the transcendental. They are not earth-bound! Every research and every earthly endeavour has a purpose but all endeavours have one ultimate goal/purpose which is not physical but spiritual or transcendental. (Integrative Humanism: Extensions and Clarifications 76)

To answer the question raised by Edet, "why then do we need to emphasize on the spiritocentric perspective?" (17), is to say that it is because the spirit is superior to the physical aspect of human being or reality. This could be the rationale behind the assertion of Ozumba and Chimakonam that "we however, stressed that in eternity we are going to have a one-valued logic as all things will be known to be true" (v). This is like saying that all will become like God who is pure Spirit in eternal. This makes God the *telos* of all existent reality. This position of the integrativists is like what Paul Tillich has argued on. Tillich posits that God as Spirit is the *telos* of life. In his words:

> Spirit is the unity of the ontological elements and the *telos* of life. Actualized as life, being-itself is fulfilled as spirit. The word *telos* expresses the relation of life and spirit more precisely... It expresses the inner directedness of life toward spirit, the urge of life to become spirit, to fulfil itself as spirit. *Telos* stands for inner, essential, necessary aim, for that in which a being fulfils its own nature. God as living is God fulfilled in himself and therefore spirit. God is spirit. (349)

In other words, all things or beings will become pure spirit, that is, one with Nke-Mbu (God), which is but pure spirit in uwa mgbe ebi-ebi – a city that is eternal (Ozumba and Chimakonam 21).

Spiritocentric Metaphysics: A Critique

The metaphysics of Ozumba's integrative humanism as stated above is spiritocentric metaphysics. It is a metaphysics that although tried to look at being and reality as having spirit and matter or spiritual and physical dimensions, but ends up giving primacy to the spiritual aspect/spirit above matter/the physical aspect of reality. This is inherent in his assertion that spirit continues to exist even at death while matter ceases to exist at this point. This connotes that spirit is eternal while matter is temporal. This conception of reality by Ozumba with respect to human being is based on Western worldview and metaphysics. It is this worldview that sees spirit as eternal and matter as temporal. Matter here is a temporal attachment to spirit which is superior and eternal.

By this, Ozumba is saying that reality is spirit and being is identical with spirit, just as Hegel identifies being with absolute spirit. It therefore follows that spirit is the essence of being since it is good while matter is not. Matter does not really constitute reality because it is bad or evil. Matter being bad or evil is not eternal, hence it ceases to exist at the death of human being. This is closely related to the platonic idea of the world of form and the physical world. The world of form is said to be the world of the good and it is eternal. While the physical world is a temporal world, of which its existence is a shadow of the real world (the world of form). This physical world is changing and not eternal, it is ephemeral. The world of form which is the real world and spiritual is what is unchanging and eternal.

Ozumba's spiritocenric metaphysics is to a reasonable extent an extension of Aristotle's bifurcating metaphysics. In Aristotle's metaphysics, it is argued that being consists of essence (substance) and accident. But Aristotle goes on to note that being can be identified with only substance, even without accident. Hence, Aristotle and Ozumba see substance and spirit as what is eternal and not temporal. They (substance and spirit) do not have any reason why not to exist even at the dissolution of being or the death of the human being. They continue to exist.

This kind of understanding of being or human being contradicts African ontology. African ontology holds that being consists of spiritual and physical aspects. In other words, being consists of spirit and matter. By instantiating or particularizing being to human being, it is posited by Terver Titus Mamadu thus, "man (is) a composite being of spiritual and material dimensions" (48). Thus, by this, African ontology does not see any point at which spirit and matter separates. If at any point they separate being ceases to exist. That is to say, if being must exist, it must exist as that which has both spiritual and physical or material dimensions. By implication, the human being cannot be associated or identified with the spiritual aspect of being alone at any point of existence. Hence, Ozumba and other integrativists cannot be right to hold that the human being continues to exist as only spiritual being at/after death.

Ozumba's spiritocentric metaphysics also contradicts the Bible which it alludes to, to substantiate its argument that 'man is a being unto eternity'. Ozumba in his writings argues that the only aspect of the human being which continues to exist unto eternity is the spiritual. This kind of position negates the biblical narrative of the translation into eternity of men such as Enoch, Elijah and Jesus Christ (Genesis 5:24; 2 Kings 2:1, 11; Acts 1:9-10). The first two men, the Bible records were taken into heaven or eternity as total beings. That is to say that they entered eternity with their soul (spirit) and body (matter). There is no part of the Bible which says that it was only their spiritual part that went into eternity. It rather holds that it is the totality of their being that was admitted into eternity. This goes as far as affirming the fact that matter and spirit are co-eternal, and continue to exist without any point of separation. It therefore makes Ozumba's spiritocentric metaphysics (philosophy) not biblical as he claims.

Another reason why Ozumba's spiritocentric metaphysics is unbiblical is because it destroys the very foundation of the resurrection and ascension of Christ. The Bible records that the body and spirit (soul) of Christ were resurrected together and that they together ascended into heaven in the person of Christ. This contradicts Ozumba's position that it is the spiritual aspect of being or the human being that continues to exist unto eternity. It rather holds that it is both matter and spirit that constitute the human being as being unto eternity. This shows that spirit and matter are co-created and co-existing for each other and will continue to exist unto eternity. Thus, each spirit (soul) has its own distinct or definite body that houses it and will continue to house it. In other words, to every soul (spirit) there is a body (matter). These two entities of the human being are inseparable. To separate them will lead to non-being. Spiritocentric metaphysics calls to question the possibility of the resurrection of Christians if one accepts that it is only spirit that is eternal. But the Christian resurrection gives the assurance that the spirit and the body of the human being will be resurrected together and will also ascend alongside each other to be with Christ in eternity. This is clearly a New Testament teaching. Ronald Nash helps to understand the stand of the New Testament on the state of the body and spirit at death and in the resurrection, as he notes that:

> The New Testament emphasizes the wholeness of the human being. The New Testament does not picture the body as a useless appendage that can be discarded. The New Testament does not teach that the body is an inferior and an unnecessary part of a human. Humans after death are not disembodied souls but rather persons, body and soul. (109)

Ozumba's spiritocentric metaphysics destroys the very essence of his philosophy, which is to care for the physical and spiritual well-being of the human being. This is apparent in Ozumba's remark which reads: "the undergirding objective of integrative humanism is the need to place man's physical and spiritual well being at the centre of every intellectual endeavour" (Philosophy and Method 19). There is no need of thinking about the well-being of both the physical and spiritual dimensions of the human being if only the spiritual will continue to exist unto eternity. This philosophy (integrative humanism) should have been concerned with human spiritual welfare or the spiritual aspect of human that transcends from this physical world to the spiritual world. But if he opines that the essence of his philosophy is to take care of the physical and spiritual well-being of human being, then his metaphysics should not be spiritocentric metaphysics. It should rather be "humanocentric metaphysics". This is because it is concerned with the well-being of the total person. Put differently, inherent in his objective is the view that both the physical and spiritual dimensions of the human being is needed for the human being to continue to exist. This can be seen in the remark of Chimakonam, which reads:

> In integrative humanism we distinguish two aspects of being (aru-physical and mmuo-spiritual), and two forms of reality (ama-ife that which appears or accident and ama-aru that which is felt or substance). In the former, the two aspects must come together for being to emerge and in the later, the two forms must come together for reality to emerge. (74)

Ozumba's idea of the human being as a being unto eternity does not hold unto this to the end. He rather identifies being with mmuo-spiritual aspect; and reality is identified with ama-aru that which is felt or substance. In all, he makes this eternal. Thus, Ozumba's spiritocentric metaphysics defeats its very goal of harmonizing the physical and transcendental, corporal and incorporal aspects of being and reality into a whole.

Conclusion

As this work comes to this stage, the questions that remain in the mind of the researcher are: has any issue on the metaphysics of integrative humanism been raised in this paper that is worthy of consideration? Or is this just a write up to add to the list of articles that are scattered in various academic journals? The researcher leaves these questions to the integrative humanists or integrativists, who may wish to clarify the researcher's worries. Indeed, integrative humanism is a dialectical philosophy that tends to say 'yes' and 'no' at the same time to a particular issue, especially with respect to the concepts of being and reality. For instance, integrative humanism tends to say that the human being consists of spirit and body (matter) but goes on to say that spirit is what really constitute the human being since it is spirit that continues to exist in eternity.

Prof. Ozumba has always left researchers and his audience in a state of perplexity whenever he has the opportunity to write or present an academic paper. This is clearly reflected in his philosophy termed 'Integrative Humanism'. He raised some puzzles on his metaphysical standpoint that has left the researcher more confused than clarified. It is so obvious in his idea that human beings consist of spirit and matter and at the same time he sees spirit as what will continue to exist in eternity without a body (matter). What a puzzle? Is it possible for spirit to exist in eternity without a body? Can someone help to unravel this puzzle to an inquiring mind?

Works Cited

Chimakonam, Jonathan Okeke. "Integrative Humanism: Extension and Clarification". *Journal of Integrative Humanism-Ghana. 3.1.* Accra: Emmpong, (May, 2013). 73-83.

Edet, Mesembe Ita. "Ozumba's Spiritocentric Humanism: A Conceptual Critique". *Journal of Integrative Humanism-Ghana. 3.1.* Accra: Emmpong, (May 2013). 3-18.

Fayerabend, Paul. *Against Method.* Ed. Furman and Avila. Caalifornia: Maryfield, 2000.

Mamadu, Terver Titus. "Integrative Humanism and the Question of Personal Identity". *Journal of Integrative Humanism-Ghana. 2.1.* Accra: Emmpong, (May 2012). 52-63.

Nash, Ronald. *Life's Ultimate Question: An Introduction to Philosophy.* Grand Rapids: Zondervan, 1999.

Okeke, Jonathan, Oduora Asuo and Sunday Agu. "Philosophy and Method of Integrative Humanism: A Response". *Journal of Integrative Humanism-Ghana. 1.1.* Accra: Emmpong, (August 2011). 49-60.

Ozumba, Godfrey Okechukwu and Jonathan Okeke Chimakonam. *Njikoka Amaka: Further Discussion on the Philosophy of Integrative Humanism (A Contribution to African and Intercultural Philosophies).* Calabar: 3rd Logic Option, 2014.

Ozumba, Godfrey Okechukwu. "Integrative Humanism and Complementary Reflection: A Comparative Analysis". *Filosofia Theoretica: An African Journal of Invention and Ideas. 1.1.* Calabar: Jochrisam, (Dec. 2011). 151-170.

---. "Integrative Humanism: The Spirit of Contemporary Philosophy". *Journal of Integrative Humanism-Ghana. 2.1.* Accra: Emmpong, (May 2012). 52-63.

---. "National Consciousness, Value Reorientation and Identity: An Integrative Humanist Approach". *Journal of Integrative Humanism-Ghana. 3.2.* Accra: Emmpong, (March 2014). 147-155.

---. "Ozumba's Spiritocentric Humanism: A Critique-A Rejoinder". *Journal of Integrative Humanism-Ghana. 3.1.* Accra: Emmpong, (May 2013). 19-27.

---. *Philosophy and Method of Integrative Humanism.* Calabar: Jochrisam, 2010.

Tillich, Paul. *Systematic Theology.* Chicago: Chicago University, 1951.

INTEGRATIVE HUMANISM AND THE METAPHYSICS OF SPIRITOCENTRICISM
BY
PROF. G.O. OZUMBA
DEPARTMENT OF PHILOSOPHY
UNIVERSITY Of CALABAR
CALABAR – NIGERIA

ABSTRACT

Integrative Humanism is a philosophy and a method of doing philosophy. It has its philosophical, scientific, psychological, spiritual, Christian, electronic, African roots. It is a philosophy with omniphilosophic and omniscientific application. Integrative humanism can be applied in all areas of disciplinary endeavours. In each context, we must understand the ratio spiritocentric bearings and import of our discourse. Our attempt here therefore is to answer some of the quandaries and issues raised by Ogbonnanya in his paper. Integrative humanism is not a wholly spiritocentric metaphysics and it does not downplay the body in preference to the soul. It rather opines that since the soul will transcend the body as it continues to exist in eternity, it deserves more attention. The soul also will exist in eternity with a body that is configured differently from its earthly body.

Key-words: *Integrative humanism, Spiritocentric metaphysics, Humanocentric metaphysics, Mundanocentric metaphysics and Bibliocentricism.*

Introduction

The debate on the many sides of integrative humanism is becoming interesting, intriguing and captivating over each passing day. As scholars reflect on the implications, interpretations and applications of the principles of integrative humanism, over a wide range of issues it throws up both needless and needful exasperations which need clarifications. One such intellectual disquisition is the questions coming from a doctoral candidate in the department of philosophy at the University of Calabar. Lucky Ogbonnaya in his article titled "A Critique of Ozumba's Spiritocentric Metaphysics" raises a number of questions namely; what is the value of spiritocentric metaphysics to the project of integrative humanism? Can we have full blooded metaphysics without a component of mundanocentric metaphysics? Is it possible to talk of spiritocentric metaphysics instead of humanocentric metaphysics that contains

13

both spiritocentric and mundanocetric dimensions of metaphysics. Finally, he asked why the spirit is regarded as supreme over and above the body. In eternity, is it possible for the human person to exist without the body? The above are some of the interpositions raised by the author in the course of his analysis of the metaphysics of integrative humanism.

Our attempt in this paper is to carry out further elucidations and classifications of some of the misgivings, doubts and issues raised by the author. It is believed that this will go a long way in addressing some of the quandaries that may be lurking in the hearts of the readers and enthusiasts of the philosophy of integrative humanism. To do justice to this essay, we need some terminological clarifications, followed by a brief purview of the canonicals of metaphysics and thereafter other incidental comments will follow.

Our Understanding of Metaphysics

The term metaphysics is derived from the classical Greek expression meta-ta-phusika meaning after the things of nature. This followed the chronicling of the books said to have been written by Aristotle by Andronicus of Rhodes Andronicus after the books that dealt with physical nature branded those with contents that border on abstract entities metaphysics which literally means "after physics", that is, books that deal with esoteric, ethereal and abstract truths. This appears to be the genesis of the confusion and interpretation of metaphysics. Metaphysics have in some quarters been interpreted as that aspect of philosophy whose subject matter must be transcendental, abstract and preternatural. But this is not so and should not be so. According to Boersema in *American Encyclopedia of Philosophy* clearly states that metaphysics is concerned primarily with the kind of things that constitute reality. This would include investigating into existences not limited to empirical, physical things but also into things outside of the senses like abstract entities (503). It also includes an investigation of questions about broader conceptions of things and reality, such things as objects or events, properties or relations. When Whitehead talks about process philosophy that constitutes creativity, change and becoming, he is well within the ambits of metaphysics. When Nelson Goodman talks about the many ways of world-making, he is talking about metaphysics, this is so because metaphysics is closely linked with ontology. Ontology simply means that branch of metaphysics concerned with being or existence in general.

The term ontology was coined by scholastic writers in the seventeen centuries. It was Rudolf Goclenius who first mentioned the word in 1636. Many have continued to use it interchangeably with metaphysics. The more acceptable construal is to see metaphysics as broader than ontology, distinguishable into rational and empirical psychology, cosmology, ontology itself and theology. Metaphysics encompasses the whole range of existent things and their many nuances, nitty gritties and extrapolations. This is why we see such metaphysicians as Meinong talking about being, non-being and becoming as co-extensive with metaphysics.

Ontology is more concerned with the concept of being qua being. It deals with the nature of existence which consists of concepts and categories in a subject area that shows the relationship between them (Oxford Advanced Learner Dictionary, 1029).

Key figures in ontology nay metaphysics will include Johannes Clauberg 1622 – 1665, Jean Baptiste Duhamel 1624-1706, Christian Gottlieb Baumgarten 1714-1762. Others will include Gottfried Leibniz and Immanuel Kant. Other ancestors of ontology will include Duns Scotus, William of Ockham, Francisco Suarez, Aquinas Anselem and others. We cannot forget the important impetus in ontological studies provided by Martin Heidegger and in contemporary time by W.V.O Quine. For Quine ontology assumes a new meaning as the determination of the range of possible potential existence that are needful in the organization and understanding of a theory. This is why he says "that to be is to be the value of a valuable"; it is our commitment to the existence of a value that makes the value of ontological significance. Thus, ontology becomes a matter of linguistics commitment and pragmatic exigency.

From our examination so far we can safely say that metaphysics embrace ontology and covers existence in all its conceivable entrails and ramification which ranges from the physical to the transcendental, seen to the unseen, abstract to the concrete. To therefore conceive metaphysics only from the abstract stand point is unacceptable.

In integrative humanism, we see integrative metaphysics as the integrated, dynamics, comprehensive and aggregated perception and study of reality in its multifarious dimensions. Reality is both extensive and complicated. It is the duty of the integrative metaphysician to be clear of what goal he is pursuing and for what purpose and then, against that background harmonizes reality to fit into that, mould for the benefit of continuing enhanced understanding of humans as beings unto eternity. We must bear in mind that our existence is with a beginning but without ending. It is always an "on-going existence" which culminates in perfect existence that remains on-going because it never ends. This leads me to further clarification of incidental terms

Clarification of terms

To further improve clarity of discourse, it is important to throw light on what we mean by mundanocentric metaphysics and spiritocentric metaphysics

Mundanocentric Metaphysics

Mundanocentricism is derived from the word "mundane", Oxford Advanced Learner's Dictionary defines mundane as "not exciting, not interesting, dull and ordinary". Generally, we take mundane to mean earthly and ordinary existence in this planet earth. Our construal in this context is the ordinary human existence that is more concerned about the satisfaction of worldly needs with no attachment to spiritual requirements.

When we therefore talk about mundanocentric metaphysics, we are talking about philosophizing that is limited to the way humans live as ordinary human beings programmed to satisfy their day to day needs. The ontological furniture needed will include the necessities of existence, housing, food, clothing, cars, social needs, economic, psychological, geological and physiological needs, etc. Man can be defined by the above needs. There are people that do not bother about spiritual needs. Like Paul the Apostle observes, their mantra is "let us eat and drink, for tomorrow we shall die". For such people what counts is the maximization of earthly comfort through acquisition of all that make life worth living, or in pursuit of certain personal goals in research, education, adventures, pleasures or other preferential legacies. Life lived this way and the incidental metaphysics will constitute what we call mundanocetric metaphysics.

Humanocentric Metaphysics

Humanocentric metaphysics differs from mundanocentricism because it is concerned about the corporate human existence as a tripartite being consisting of soul, spirit and body. Every human being has the spiritual and the physical dimensions. This makes man to always ask questions about his physical and spiritual wellbeing. A man/woman has body and needs to care about the things that concern his body. Likewise he has spirit and needs to also take care of the spiritual needs.

What makes man (as a generic term) is that man is human and continues as human on earth or in heaven/eternity. This appears to be the crux of the matter. Does man continue to exist as human in eternity and if he does, does he live in eternity with the earthly body or with a different body or does he exist as a disembodied spirit in eternity?

There exist some conflicting signals from African traditional system and some Christian beliefs. There is therefore need to explicate these tangles to straighten the facts and clear the doubts and misgivings.

Spiritocentric metaphysics

Spiritocentric metaphysics is concerned about metaphysics of spiritual reality or what we may call transcendental metaphysics. Man is a being unto eternity and that means that he first exists as an earthly being (on probation) and then translates to the eternal plane fondly called "the great beyond", "heaven", "hell", paradise or eternity. The Holy writ contains the facts about the nature of that existence. According to how we have lived on earth, we may find ourselves either on the blissful side of eternity (heaven) or on the bleak side of eternity (hell). In eternity (whether hell or heaven) existence is real with all the appropriate appurtenance and furniture for that realm of existence. We talk of God, angels, cherubims, seraphims, trees, rivers, streets made of gold, etc. On the other hand, we have lucifer, devils, demons and other doleful creatures and dismal environment. We have accepted bibliocentricism because it is from the bible which is God's manual to man that we can get the truth about the profile for earthly and eternal existence. We need not speculate outside the confines of God's revelational knowledge.

Our interlocutor raises the question of whether in spiritocentric metaphysics the soul does not have a body? Does the soul or spirit exist in disembodied form? He alluded to the African traditional belief system where souls are said to retain their earthly body. Ancestors are said to retain their bodies, Abiku (Ogbanje) children keep reincarnating with their bodies as is believed in African traditional system.

The Holy writ has an answer to the quandary expressed above. In first Corinthians, chapter fifteen, verse thirty-five to forty-four (1cor. 15:35-44), it explains: "But some man will say, how are the dead raised up? And with what body do they come? Thou fool, that which thou sowest is not quickened, except it die: And that which thou sowest, thou sowest not that body that shall be, but bare grain, it may chance of wheat, or some other grain: But God giveth it a body... All flesh is not the same flesh, but there is one kind of flesh of men, another flesh of beast, another of fishes, and another of birds, there are also celestial bodies and bodies terrestrial; but the glory of the celestial is one, and the glory of the terrestrial is another... So also is the resurrection of the dead. It is sown in corruption, it is raised in incorruption: It is sown in dishonour, it is raised in glory; it is sown in weakness; it is raised in power. It is sown a natural body; it is raised a spiritual body. There is a natural body and there is a spiritual body".

The Holy writ goes on to clarify with the following words "behold I shew you a mystery: we shall not all sleep [die] but we shall all be changed. In a moment, in the twinkling of an eye, at the last trump; for the trumpet shall sound and the dead shall be raised incorruptible, and we shall be changed. For this corruptible must put on incorruption and this mortal must put on immortality" (verses 51 – 53).

The above excerpts from the Holy book throw light on the truth. To appreciate and understand the nature of the soul's spiritual body, we must underscore God's omnipotence. God can do all things in a twinkle of an eye. Our problems begin when we either want to understand the whole of reality with our limited cognitive capacity or when we insist on interpreting all reality from a circumscribed physicalistic view point. This is why the Holy book says that "secret things belong to God but revealed things belong to us" (Deut. 29:29) and the book of Job further says "can man by searching find God?" (Job 11:7). This is the essence of integrative humanism, to wit, to integrate the physical with the spiritual. And this is why we emphasize bibliocentricism as the source of our inspiration and enlightenment.

From the foregoing, it is clear that in eternity (after death) the soul or spirit still has a body appropriate to its ethereal existence but the physical body is temporarily discarded. On the resurrection, the spiritual body will once again be re-united with a spiritually refurnished, reinvigorated and renewed old body. This is clearly stated in Isaiah 26: 19 that "thy dead men shall live, together with my dead body shall they arise" further in John's gospel the Holy book states:

> Marvel not at this, for the hour is coming in which all that are in the graves shall hear his voice. And shall come forth, they that have done good, unto the resurrection of life and they that have done evil unto the resurrection of damnation (John 5: 28-29).

The above quotation confirms the eventual union of the spiritualized body of the soul with the spiritualized and refurnished discarded body, forming a new self that will live in the millennium and in eternity as the case may be.

This means that spiritocentric metaphysics does not down play the importance of the physical body but only deprecates it exaltation above the spiritual component of man. The spirit man remains more important than the physical man of mere flesh and blood. What we seek to achieve in line with the Berkeleyean view point is to stress the folly of paying all attention to man's physical existence with no or minimal regard to the spirit man which will outlive the body (in its present nature). Integrative humanism presses the importance of a good earthly existence and a good eternal existence. These two must be metaphysically integrated in our pursuits in order to have a lasting and fulfilling existence. Spiritocentricism is thereof humanocentric and mundanocentric. There cannot be a worthy spiritocentric existence without a worthy mundane and human existence. But after the earthly existence man ceases to be mere human, he becomes super-human or spirit-human, still having spirit and body but now with spiritualized nature.

African World-View and Eternity

Africans believed that man in this physical world has the physical and spiritual dimensions of his being. The spiritual is what leaves the body when he is asleep; it is what is involved in astral travel, witchcraft activity and other sundry functions. The human person is believed to have part of his beingness coming from his paternal, maternal, cultural and divine origins. And this makes man to be inextricably connected with their ancestral lines or lineage. Eternity for the Africans end in a life that is continued with good and praiseworthy ancestors in the spiritual world prepared for those who live good lives while those that lived evil lives continued as malignant and roaming spirits. It is believed that dead humans whether as good ancestors or bad spirits still affect the living and can be consulted to either help the living or invoked to carryout evil assignment for the living who employ their services.

The truth of dispensationalism tells us of ever increasing revelation. God is in the business of unveiling secret truths to mankind. The coming of Christianity marks another epoch of revelational unveiling of further truths which supercedes and sheds light on the dark corners of African traditional belief. The so-called malignant or evil spirits are demonic spirits which constitute part of fallen angels that rebelled against God. They have the power to manipulate, orchestrate and take on different forms in the course of their sole functions which are to deceive, confuse, mislead, entrap and destroy. What the traditional African thinks is ancestral spirit is a malignant devil that transforms into the image of a dead family member supposedly called an ancestor. The Holy writ says that "it is appointed unto all men once to die and after that the judgment" (Heb 9:27). The idea therefore that humans die and continue to live with their body is false. It will be at the time of resurrection which is yet for the future. Integrative mind-set anticipates our translation from the traditional African mind-set to the Christian mind-set so as to imbue in us well aligned truth about humanocentric and spiritocentric metaphysics.

Conclusion

We have tried to throw light on the issues raised by Ogbonnaya to educate us on what spiritocentric metaphysics as an aspect of integrative humanist metaphysics is all about. As we have stated, spiritocentric metaphysics is only an aspect of the metaphysics that we have to deal with. Integrative humanism articulates all other aspects of metaphysics like scientific, phenomenological, existential, idealistic, realistic, Marxist, capitalist, ethical, naturalist, or any other metaphysics. What is important for the integrative humanist is to integrate all relevant insights, spiritual or physical in our understanding, and explication in the application of research search lights. We have by this exposition laid to rest the unremitting misconception that integrative humanism is wholly a spiritocentric affair.

Works Cited

Boersema, David "Metaphysics" in *American Encyclopedia of Philosophy* edited. John Lach and Robert Talisee 2008 edition.

Mesembe, Edet "Godfrey Ozumba's Spiritocentris Humanism: A Conceptual Critique". In the *Journal of Integrative Humanism.* Vol. 3, No1, 2013.

Ozumba, G.O. *The Philosophy and Method of Integrative Humanism*, Calabar: Jochrisam publishers 2010.

Ozumba, G.O. "Ozumba's Spiritocentric Humanism: A conceptual Critique: a Rejoinder" *The Journal of Integrative Humanism* Vol. 3 No 2. 2014.

Ozumba, G.O. and Jonathan Chimakoham. *Njikoka Amaka: Further Discussions on the Philosophy of Integrative Humanism*. London 3rd Logic Option, 2014.

Ozumba, G.O. *Understanding the Philosophy of W.V.O Quine* Calabar: Samroi publishers, 2003.

King James Version of the Holy Bible.

Wash, W.H. "Metaphysics, Nature of" in *Encyclopedia of Philosophy*, Vols 5 and 6, Ed. Paul Edwards, 2004 edition.

FROM AFRICAN LOGIC TO THE DEVELOPMENT OF TRADITIONS OF LOGIC IN AFRICAN PHILOSOPHY: AN INTEGRATIVIST PERSPECTIVE

BY

V. C. A NWEKE
DEPARTMENT OF PHILOSOPHY
UNIVERSITY OF CALABAR
nwekevca@gmail.com

ABSTRACT

Logic appositely understood as the study of the principles that enable human beings to think soundly, judge distinctly, communicate effectively and act appropriately is essentially a product of reason and the fact that every individual is endowed with reason shows that logic is a natural appurtenance of human nature and as such exists in all cultures. The laws of logic are therefore the universal rules of valid human thought processes which make it possible for human beings from different cultures to communicate and relate intelligibly with each other. Against this backdrop, this paper argues that the question of the logical ability of the African is a sort of intellectual disquiet that is naturally unfounded and that the existence of African philosophy as an academic field of study is an indisputable evidence that the African is as logical as any other human being. Hence, the logic question in African philosophy in the 21st century should be concerned with how to redefine, discover and develop new laws and systems of logic that will help Africans and other human beings to think, judge, evaluate, act and relate better with nature, discover innovational theories, invent new wonderful technologies, meet their needs, transform their societies and co-exist peacefully in their multi-cultural societies. Ultimately, the paper concludes that the development of viable systems of logic in African philosophy is a feasible and plausible project that should be done through a conscious search, articulation and conversational presentation of alternative systems of logic in African philosophy for the intellectual scrutiny of logicians and not through a critical, apologetic, reactionary and ethnocentric debate on the existence of a distinct African logic that is different from the universal human thought processes. The paper adopts the method of integrative humanism in its arguments and propositions.

Key-words: *Logic, African Philosophy, African Logic, Integrative Humanism, Human Thought Processes*

Introduction

African philosophy as a distinct academic enterprise was erected through decades of serious intellectual debate. Erudite professionally trained philosophers of African origin and their non-African colleagues dissipated a lot

22

of intellectual resources at their disposal arguing for the existence and non-existence of African philosophy (Okolo, 9, Momoh, Substance of African Philosophy 1). Thus unlike the early beginning of Western or any other regional philosophy, African philosophy as a professional discipline started with "metaphilosophical issues" – "Tied in with its early beginning is a long drawn-out debate over its nature, possibility, scope, and even composition" (Asiegbu,39). As a result of this, African philosophy was for a very long time focused on a sort of cultural excavation of the philosophical thoughts of traditional Africans on the one hand, and the historical excavation of the truth about the origin of philosophy on the other hand. This excavation culminated into the argument that philosophy originated from Africa, a position that is veraciously buttressed in George G.M. James' revolutionary book; *The Stolen Legacy* and Innocent I. Onyewuenyi's masterpiece; *The African Origin of Greek Philosophy: An Exercise in Afrocentrism.*

To state that the above project and discovery has lots of merits is to state the obvious. But in spite of its merits, its major disadvantage is that it reduced the scope of African philosophy to the status of a reactionary and backward looking discipline that tends to be insensitive to the present philosophical needs of the world, ignores the situation in contemporary Africa, as well as being indifferent to the future direction of African philosophy (Ozumba, The Spirit Contemporary African Philosophy, 2-6). It was after the demise of the controversy on African philosophy that professional African philosophers began to call for, and strive to chart a new direction for African philosophy as a critical, systematic and conversational discipline that is dedicated to the present philosophical needs of the world, engages the present condition and directs the aspirations of Africa/ns towards the construction, adoption or adaptation of adequate socioeconomic, political, nay scientifico-technological ideologies, systems, doctrines or philosophy that will accelerate the progressive transformation of their societies for human well being ((Oladipo, 7-32). This task ultimately calls for system building in African philosophy. And some African philosophers have channeled their intellectual erudition towards this project. Thus the emergence of different philosophical systems in contemporary African philosophy such as Asouzu's *Complementary Reflection* or *Ibuanyidanda Philosophy,* Ozumba's *Integrative Humanism,* Ijiomah's *Harmonious Monism,* and Essien's *Compatibility Theory* (See Asouzu, Ibuanyidanda: Special Edition, 1).

Consequently, this short essay argues that the development of the branches of African philosophy, specifically logic should not toe the reactionary, apologetic and ethnocentric route that delayed the emergence of a vibrant African philosophy for many decades. It challenges African philosophers with a penchant for logic to consciously articulate, rigorously systematize and conversationally present viable traditions of logic in African philosophy, traditions or systems of logic that will enable Africans and indeed similarly situated people to solve certain problems and as well embody the universal principles of logic (Ozumba and Chimakonam, 1). In doing this, we adopt integrative humanism as a method "of bringing a new understanding to bear on old facts" (Ozumba, Integrative Humanism, 23). Our ultimate objective is to use integrative humanism as a tool for sifting and welding old facts and contending positions concerning the development of *African logic* into a better and more acceptable harmonious position. To wit, we begin with the question: "what is logic?"

What is Logic?

Etymologically, the English word logic is said to be derived from a meaning-laden Greek word *logos*, a word that has been translated to mean sentence, discourse, reason, rule, account, rational, principles and definition (Uduma, Introduction to Logic, 1). Although this etymological account does not make the subject matter of logic vivid, it nonetheless shows that the English words, logic, reason, and language have the same Greek word, *logos*, as their etymological root. It therefore unveils the necessary affinity between logic, reason and language. Logic is indeed a product of reason, and its fundamental nature is communicated through language; yet it is reason and logic that make language possible and intelligible (Asouzu, Logic and Language, 75-79, Sanguineti, 21-23). Besides, the traditional "purpose of logic is to evaluate real arguments in natural languages" (Cook, 174). Against this backdrop, C. S. Momoh rightly argues that in a sense:

> ... logic relates to how critical, discriminating, rational and reasonable the normal average human being is in discussion, discourse and arguments. In this first sense, logic is concerned with the *clarity of expression, coherence and consistency, and the avoidance of vagueness, ambiguity and fallacies and contradictions.* In everyday usage of natural language, we talk of a person as being logical if he is *reasonable, sensible, fair and intelligent,* if he can unemotionally and critically distil evidence or a situation, if he can avoid contradiction, lies, inconsistency and

incoherence or if he can hold a point of view, argue for and from it, summon counter-examples and answer objections (Elements of Formal Logic, 203-4).

The basic import from the above elucidation is that logic is fundamentally an appurtenance of human nature. The human person as a being endowed with reason is logical by nature. And since "reason" is, as Rene Descartes opines, "the most equally distributed in all human beings" (1), it necessarily follows that logic is "an attribute of every competent individual" (Momoh, The Logic Question, 180). "On the basis of this observation, no human being per se is devoid of fundamental, natural logical disposition" (Asouzu, Logic and Language,75). The natural logical disposition in question is the ability to think distinctly, talk coherently, argue consistently, judge soundly, and act appropriately. What this comes to is that logic is the principle of intelligibility. It is that which enables the human mind to "represent the world to itself in a coherent, ordered, consistent and intelligible manner" (Asouzu, Logic and Language, 76) through language.

At this point, one discovers that logic primarily deals with arguments. Logic, both as a natural disposition and a formal discipline, is basically concerned with the evaluation of the product of human reasoning. In other words, the subject matter of logic is the evaluation of arguments or the justification of judgment (Uduma, Symbolic Logic, 1, 2, Bonachristus, 1-3, 9). And since every judgment and indeed every "argumentation tries to bring together statements with an eye on their unique connectivity", C. O. Ijiomah posits that logic deals with the relation between propositions (statements) that make up an argument or judgment (An Excavation, 19).This is the case because the interest of a logician while evaluating arguments is either with the syntactic relation or with the semantic relation between propositions. While formal logic is exclusively concerned with the syntactic relation, that is, the formal structure or form of valid arguments, informal/material logic is concerned with the semantic relation as well, that is, the factual meaning and content of arguments. It studies meaning in general, of ordinary words as well as of formal words like 'all', 'and', 'some, 'if ... then' etc., and of both words and sentences and this broadens into the study of language in general: how it does what it does and how it relates to the world (Lacey, 185). Appositely, the various strands of logic can be broadly grouped into formal logic and informal logic. Thus, Dale Jacquette, after acknowledging the problematique of defining logic audaciously states:

A working definition that may be correct ... is to say that logic in any of its manifestation is the systematic study of principles of correct reasoning. The principles of logic can be explored formally or informally, and by any of a number of different styles of exposition which may be highly specialized in dealing with very particular areas of reasoning. Logic is both a symbolism for the expression of the formal structures of thought and an inference mechanism for calculating and drawing assumptions in reasoning (2).

Be this as it may, logic as the study of the universal laws of human thought processes or the fundamental principles of correct reasoning deals with the formal structure of valid arguments. And the aspect of logic that deals exclusively with the formal structure of arguments is formal logic. This is because formal logic has no interest whatsoever in the content of arguments. It is concern with the relations between propositions and not their factual meaning. All it asks is whether the conclusion of an argument is entailed by its premises. It does not ask whether the premises are true (Bonachristus, 8). For instance, in formal logic, the argument:

"All bachelors are married men
Peter is a bachelor
Therefore Peter is a married man"

is as valid (logically true) as the argument:

"All bachelors are unmarried men
Peter is a bachelor
Therefore Peter is an unmarried man".

This is the case because (in spite of the apparent contradiction between the meaning of the propositions that make up the first argument) both of the arguments have the same form:

All s is p
r is s
Therefore r is p.

The off-shot of this is that logic in the strict modern sense is a "theory of formal inference" (Uduma, Introduction to Logic, 245). According to Ruch, some logicians such as Bochenski restrict the scope of logic to formal logic. In a sense, Ruch's elucidation on Bochenski's idea of logic is a vivid description of formal logic. Here is a long citation from Ruch's analysis:

For him [Bochenski] logic is a purely formal science which investigates the process of inferring universally and necessarily valid statements. This cannot involve the matter of such statements but only their necessary formal relationship. Thus formal logic constitutes the formal basis of deductive inferential knowledge and even investigates formal transformations and substitutions of reductive propositions into deductive ones. It concerns itself with how to think inferentially, not with what to think. This purely mental gymnastics is ofcourse, not everybody "cup of tea." … Formal logic is therefore a relatively sterile game which builds coherent systems of interrelated forms of expression without concerning itself with their material meaning, thus meriting the famous gibe of Russell: "In logic we never know what we are talking about nor whether what we say is true" (267).

The point here is that formal logic is concern with the universal form of valid arguments. And since what determines the validity of arguments is its form/structure independent of contents/meaning, formal logic makes use of symbols so that it can be able to capture the form/structure as well as aid logicians to evaluate the validity of arguments without knowing their factual contents. Indeed, through the help of symbols, logicians have been able to unveil the formal relations between propositions, discover, and prescribe the universal rules of valid inference as well as the rules that govern the transformation of arguments from a natural language into a rationally planned artificial language (Uduma, Symbolic Logic, 26, Ruch, 257-62). In this sense, formal logic is said to be symbolic, deductive, rational and artificial. For formal logic is carried out in a rationally planned artificial language that is fixed, consistent, symbolic, deductive, and culture independent. Hence while informal logic is natural and inherent in every human being, formal logic is artificial and as such can only be used by one who has mastered its techniques through formal education (Momoh, The Logic Question, 180). A competent logician can use the rules of formal logic to adequately transform, symbolize, and evaluate the validity of arguments expressed in any human language. This is because the rules of formal logic are the rules of universal formal inference.

From a Debate on African Logic to the Development of Traditions of Logic

The existence of African philosophy has led scholars to call for the development of the branches of African philosophy. C. B. Okolo argues that: "Although the African perceives his world in its totality, it is usually and objectively differentiated in parts. Consequently, reflection on it should be done in parts. Like all other philosophies, therefore, African philosophy has major parts or branches" (13). Sequel to this submission, Okolo itemize the major branches of African philosophy to include: Logic, Metaphysics, Ethics, Political Philosophy, Aesthetics, Epistemology and what he called "Departmental (African) Philosophies" – Philosophy of African Disciplines, namely, "Philosophy of African Language, Philosophy of African Religion, Philosophy of African History, Philosophy of African Education, and Philosophy of African Culture" (13-18). Similarly, Panteleon Iroegbu, in his book entitled *Enwisdomization and African Philosophy* agrees with Okolo's submission. For him, the main branches or compartments under which African philosophy could be developed and studied are: Logic, Metaphysics, Epistemology, Ethics, Cosmology, Anthropology, Socio-Political Philosophy, Axiology, Aesthetics, Hermeneutic/Linguistic Philosophy, Psychology and History of Philosophy (135-138).

Furthermore, Okolo and Iroegbu in their respective works posit that logic is in a fundamental sense, the *soul of philosophy* and as such should be given serious attention in African philosophy. Okolo argument is that logic is "perhaps, the most important and fundamental branch of philosophy" because "all branches of philosophy indeed employ thinking" but "Whether the type of thinking is correct or not depends on whether it is in accord with the laws of logic." – For, "Logic, usually defined as the study of ideal method in techniques of reasoning ... is that branch of philosophy which reflects upon thought and the nature of thinking itself... Every philosophical system therefore must have logic" (13). Base on this position, Okolo rhetorically elucidates:

> What about African philosophy? Is there such a thing as a different kind of mental process for Africans? Thinking as such is a property of all men, of all races and of all times. There is no such thing as a pre-logical stage of human development. Every language has its own inner logic and all races think logically. The differences are of degree not kind. Consequently, there is no question of African logic as distinct in kind from western logic, for example... (13).

The point on prominent relief here is that logicality is an inherent feature of human nature and that human thought processes are universally the same. Thus, the laws of logic are universal. Different systems of logic interpret and apply the same laws of logic in different contexts. Though some systems of logic are more sophisticated than others, but the syntactic rules governing their structure are all based on the universal laws of human thought processes. Thus, African logic should not be the study and development of the laws of the thought processes of Africans from a unique and distinct African thought system that is separate from the universal laws of human thought processes. Seen in this perspective, there is no distinct African logic just as there is neither a distinct Oriental nor Western logic derived from the laws of a peculiar Oriental or Western thought system whose laws are distinct from the universal laws of human thought processes (Uduma, Between Universalism and Cultural Identity, 1).

Contrary to this position, Udo Etuk (98-116) and Jonathan Okeke Chimakonam (141-152) concurring with Ijiomah (Revisited, 97-8) that there is a substantial difference between African Logic and Western Logic argue for a distinct and unique African Logic. Chimakonam went as far as announcing a debate on the possibility of a peculiar African Logic (141-2). He maintains that "modus ponens and indeed all the inferential rules which have material implication as major operator do not hold in African thought system" (149). If this view is correct, then the call for a distinct African Logic is flawless. An analysis of the examples Chimakonam employed to buttress his claim prove the contrary – that modus ponens and all the inferential rules which have material implication as its major operator do hold in African thought system. To wit, an analysis of the major example Chimakonam use to buttress his point is necessary.

Using characters in the monumental novel of the renowned cerebral Igbo scholar, Chinua Achebe, *Things Fall Apart*, Chimakonam, presents the following two arguments|:

1.   Every citizen of Umuofia must join the queue to be served. Unoka is a citizen of Umuofia. Therefore, Unoka must join the queue to be served.

2.   Every citizen of Umuofia must join the queue to be served. Ezeudu is a citizen of Umuofia. Therefore, Ezeudu must join the queue to be served.

According to Chimakonam, though the above arguments have the same form, going by Igbo custom, the first argument is valid but the second is not. This is because Ezeudu, unlike Unoka, is a title man and going by the "Custom" of Igbo people a title man and an "ordinary" man are not equal. Hence Ezeudu can never be asked to queue behind an "ordinary" man (149).

Every good student of logic knows that Chimakonam introduced something else that is not contained in the argument – the *status condition*. And this is where the problem lies. In fact, going by the rules of formal logic, both arguments are valid. Even an untutored African will attests to this if the arguments are properly couched to include the missing part Chimakonam introduced in his analysis. Thus we can properly present the arguments thus:

1.   Every citizen of Umuofia that is not a title holder must join the queue to be served.

Unoka is a citizen of Umuofia and he is not a title holder. Therefore, Unoka must join the queue to be served.

2.   Every citizen of Umuofia that is not a title holder must join the queue to be served. Ezeudu is a citizen of Umuofia and he is a title holder. Therefore, Ezeudu must not join the queue to be served.

A competent individual from any culture can establish the validity of these arguments. But since formal logic in its strict modern sense is essentially hypothetical and propositional in contrast to traditional formal logic which is essentially categorical and syllogistic. (Uduma Introduction to Logic, 245-48, Sanguineti, 33,109, Ruch , 239) the above arguments can be further reformulated and couched in a hypothetical, nay propositional form, thus:

1.   If every citizen of Umuofia that is not a title holder must join the queue to be served and Unoka is a citizen of Umuofia and he is not a title holder then Unoka must join the queue to be served.

2.   If every citizen of Umuofia that is not a title holder must join the queue to be served and Ezeudu is a citizen of Umuofia and he is a title holder, then Ezeudu must not join the queue to be served.

Using "C" to represent a citizen of Umuofia "T" to represent a title holder, and "Q" to represent must join the queue, the above arguments can be schematically presented in propositional logic as thus:

(1).   1. $(C .-T) \rightarrow Q$ (2).   1. $(C . -T) \rightarrow Q$

         2. $C . -T /\!\!\cdot Q$ 2. $C . T / \cdot -Q$

Contrary to the position of Chimakonam, any individual who has mastered the techniques of formal logic can appropriately evaluate the validity of these arguments using the rules of formal logic including modus ponens and indeed all other rules of inference that have material implication as a major operator. This idea is neither novel nor news. It has been buttressed and substantiated in the works of many erudite African scholars such as Makinde (1978, 1989 and 2010), Momoh (1989) 2000 and 2005), Etuk (2002), Enyimba (2005) and Jaja and Badey 2012) – just to list a few. The common point envisaged and demonstrated in all of these works is that the rules of formal logic can be used to evaluate arguments in African philosophy, worldview or culture. Hence the idea that Africans have a different thought process that is either inferior or superior to that of other people is false. This can also be illustrated by analyzing the conversation between the Duke of She (European) and Confucius (Chinese) which Etuk quotes from Russell on "Chinese Morals" to buttress the need for a peculiar African logical structure. The passage, which began with the Duke of She addressing Confucius, reads:

> "We have an upright man in our country. His father stole a sheep and the son bore witness against him."
>
> "In our country", Confucius replied, "uprightness is something different from this. A father hides the guilt of his son and a son hides the guilt of his father. It is in such conduct that true uprightness is to be found" (Etuk, 98).

The position of Chimakonam and Etuk that the above conversation suggests that the validity of the position of the Duke of She and that of Confucius depend on different logical structures is not correct. The correct thing to say is that they argue from different premises base on their different beliefs. But both arguments can be evaluated using the same logical structure. Thus we have the following:

1. An upright person bear true witness even against his family members
   Thomas' father stole a sheep and Thomas bore witness against.
   Therefore Thomas is an upright person.

2. An upright person hide the guilt of his family members
   Thomas' father stole a sheep and Thomas hid the guilt of his father
   Therefore Thomas is an upright person.

At this point one notices that though the propositions that make up the above two arguments are different and that both arguments make use of different standards of uprightness, the structure of the two arguments are the same and both arguments are valid. What this shows is that the structure of valid arguments is universal. The corollary of this is that the content of human thoughts do differ from one culture to another but the structure of human thought processes are universal. Thus, systems or traditions of logic in African philosophy must be base on the universal laws of human thought processes. Against this backdrop, we submit that it is wrong to do logic using geographical categorization – "African logic", Western logic", "Igbo logic", "Eastern logic". For this approach erroneously mislead people to conclude that the thought processes of different people are different from that of others and that a people living within the same geographical location necessarily think and act in the same way (Asouzu, Some Basic Philosophical Problems, 93-4).

This position far from suggesting the logical incapacity of the African or that logic cannot be a legitimate branch of African philosophy admits that Africans are as logical as any other human being and as such logic as a branch of philosophy should not be develop along racial lines; along the ethnocentric division between logical and pre-logical mentality or between a superior and inferior thought system. Logic as a branch of African philosophy should concern itself with the study, discovery, development, reinterpretation, and appropriation of the universal laws of human thought processes in order to construct better systems of logic that will help Africans, nay any human being, in and from any race, to interact with the universe, think clearly, judge soundly, act appropriately, explore and exploit nature in better ways for human well being. In line with this point of view, Okolo avers:

> African logic has ... meaning in the sense that logic deals with thinking, language, or inference and these are usually with one's world or culture. There is a bond between language and culture, thinking and its object... African logic or logic in African philosophy is concerned not with the very thinking processes of the African, the realm of pure logic but its application to the world and culture of the African, to his language and objects of his reference. This is clearly seen in his social discourse and interactions, land disputes, family feuds or in any social event where speeches orations are needed. One sees here the working of the African mind, its inner logic, consistency, its rich language and imagery. African logic therefore is a legitimate inquiry in philosophy (14).

What the foregoing comes to is that African logic as a legitimate branch of African philosophy is not concern with the study of the thinking processes of the African in order to discover and develop the ideal laws of the thought processes of Africans distinct from the universal laws of human thought processes; rather, it is the application of the universal laws of human thought processes to the African world and culture in an intelligible and systematic manner. This conception of African logic projects the plausible route to doing logic in African philosophy.

Accordingly, U. O. Uduma suggests that one of the areas that logic in African philosophy can contribute to the global growth of logic is in the area of dialectical logic, and that: "Africans must not border themselves about formulating artificially regulated logistic language. Logic is not exhausted in formal logic; indeed formal logic is only a tiny aspect of logic" (African Logic, 289). In as much as the above position is true, we maintain that Africans can still contribute to the development of formal logic. This is because formal logic is not yet a complete system. The scope of logic as a legitimate branch of African philosophy includes the development and systematization of alternative systems of logic. C. S. Momoh in the last part of his very important paper "The Logic Question in African Philosophy" argues that "developments in formal logic may never be complete" and that "what is likely to happen is that a new system equally related to thinking and reasoning will be discovered and developed..." (186). Hence, he concludes that:

> ... even though it is possible to use existing formal logics and rules of inference to evaluate discourse, reasoning and thoughts in African cultures, and world-views the authentic African logic in African logistic language is yet to be developed. African professional philosophers have this gauntlet to pick up (187).

The point underscored here is that there is a strong link between logic and language. And just as every culture has its natural language; a rationally planned artificial logistic language can be develop from any given natural language. M. A. Makinde, in his paper entitled "The Question of African Philosophy" concurs with Momoh's position by arguing that every valid form of human reasoning carried out in all human languages observes the universal laws governing human thought processes. The import of this is that "the fundamental principles of logic need not be learned by, or taught to, people before they could reason logically" (42). Furthermore, he contends:

> Because of its assumed universal validity and applicability in all thoughts, logic, like mathematics, cannot be relativised. As there is no American or African mathematics, there is

nothing to be called American or African logic, otherwise it would no longer be true that the principles of logic are assumed in all rational thought, a condition that applies without discrimination to all people. They, of course, would not be known as human beings but beasts to whom the above condition does not apply. It is one of the conditions by which we differentiate human beings from the lower animals, and that is why language is an important part of logic and reasoning. Where you have language, there is logic, and where you have logic, there is language (42).

The implication of this is that since there is African language, there is African logic, and if there is African logic, such logic can be represented in a rationally planned logistic language. But does this mean that Makinde is contradicting his position about the universality of logic? The answer to this question is an emphatic NO! This is because every rationally planned logistic language has the same form and follows the same universal principles of logic. Accordingly, Mankinde vividly posits:

Therefore if the principle of logic are universal in all human beings capable of thinking in a human language, coherent logical systems could be built in all human languages, insofar as such languages not only perform the expressive and communicative, but also the descriptive and argumentative functions. For instance, Modus Ponens, a valid principle of inference, would be recognized as such in any African thought system. The same could be said of other logical principles, including the fundamental laws of thought... What is true of the above laws or principles of logic will be true of all principles of valid inference (42).

The basic position espoused here is that there is no peculiar African logical structure of thought distinct from the universal structure of valid human thought processes. What this mean is that the development of logic in African philosophy should gear towards appropriating, possibly, redefining existing fundamental principles of logic or even discover additional ones, for the construction of better systems of logic and in so doing contribute meaningfully to the universal development of logic. Owing to this, we submit that it is more appropriate to talk of "Logic in African Philosophy" or "Traditions of Logic in African Philosophy" as against "African Logic". M. I. Edet has in his interesting paper, *Metaphysics, Contemporary African Philosophy and*

Ethnocentric Commitment, argues veraciously that the concept "African Metaphysics" is an inappropriate caption for doing metaphysics in African philosophy, he, perhaps intentionally, failed to show that the same applies to logic (113-115), which is the most universal branch of philosophy. In this regard, we posit that the development of traditions of logic in African philosophy demand that we shift from the debate on African logic to a conscious articulation of traditions of logic in African philosophy.

The Plausible Route to the Development of Traditions of Logic in African Philosophy

One of the basic features of African philosophy both in the past and in the present is its apparent "apathy towards system building and development" (Akpan, 589). The major cause of this situation is the fact that the first team of professional philosophers of African origin dissipated their resources – time, and energy – debating on the existence of African philosophy without constructing viable philosophical systems upon which later generation of African philosophers will build on. They were more or less doing African philosophy, albeit indirectly, and as such were unable to rise beyond the first and second level of doing philosophy – the stage of criticism and the stage of hermeneutic engagement – to the highest level of doing philosophy, the level of synthesis and system building (Oguejiofor, 6-21).

The point of prominent relief here is that we may spend a lot time, dissipating lots of energy debating on African logic without developing any system or tradition of logic in African philosophy. Thus the discovery, systematization and progressive emendation of viable traditions of logic in African philosophy will hardly emerge by debating on the existence, possibility or nonexistence of traditions of logic in African philosophy, the best option is to consciously start constructing, systematizing, and presenting traditions of logic in African philosophy using the universal laws of human thought processes. The import of this is that the plausible route to the development of traditions of logic in African philosophy should be neither apologetic nor ethnocentric.

The viable traditions of logic in African philosophy that are gradually germinating are products of cross-cultural fertilization, rigorous construction and conversational presentation. To be specific, some members of the Calabar School of Philosophy are consciously and critically researching, redefining, articulating, systematizing, and presenting new laws of logic, nay different traditions/systems of logic – that can fall within the universal canopy of human thought processes – in an objective and conversational manner. This new laudable approach is evident not only in Chris Ijiomah's *Harmonious Monism* (Contemporary Views, 43-50, An Excavation, 32-4) and, Innocent Asouzu's *Complementary/Ibuanyidanda Logic* (Method and Principles, 348-54, Ibuanyidanda 70-80, Some Basic Philosophical Problems, 90-104)but also in Jonathan Chimakonam's *Ezumezu Logic* (The Criteria and Some Contemporary Methods). Although these systems are still ongoing projects, it is now the duty of the intellectual community, especially students of the Calabar School of Philosophy, to nurture, groom, fertilize, refine and further develop these traditions through critical scrutiny and in so doing contribute to the development of viable systems of logic in African Philosophy.

Conclusion

The main point buttressed in this article is that the approach of Udo Etuk's "The Possibility of African Logic"; and Jonathan Chimakonam's "Why Can't There be an African Logic" to the development of African logic is reactionary, apologetic and ethnocentric and as such inadequate. The emergence of viable systems of logic in African philosophy will come through the act of rigorous construction, conversational presentation, incessant emendation, novel interpretation, discovery and application of new, nay existing laws/systems of logic.

In sum, we conclude that logic is though a universal discipline and the laws of formal logic are the universal laws of human thought processes; its application differ from one context to another. Thus what logicians have been doing is to construct logical systems that can help them to explore, explain, evaluate and exploit certain aspects of reality to solve a given problem. African logicians can and should do same when and where necessary. The laws of valid human thought processes are universal but more can still be discovered, and they are, have and can be used to develop different systems of logic that serves the different needs of human beings in different societies, at different epochs. Reality is still unfolding!

Works Cited

Akpan, Chris O. "The Yesterday and Today of African Philosophy: Towards New Prospects." *From Footmarks to Landmarks on African Philosophy* Andrew F. Uduigwomen Ed. Lagos: Obaroh and Ogbinaka Publishers, 2009.

Asiegbu, Martins F. "African Philosophy: Problems, Debates, Approaches, and Challenges. *Flash: Journal of Philosophy and Religion,* 2.1. (2008), 38-49.

Asouzu Innocent, *The Method and Principles of Complementary in and Beyond African Philosophy,* Calabar: University of Calabar Press, 2004.

Asouzu Innocent, "Logic and Language" In: Asouzu I. Innocent. *Ikwa Ogwe: Essential Readings in Complementary Reflection. A Systematic Methodological Approach,* Calabar: Saesprint Publishers, 2007.

Asouzu Innocent, *Ibuanyidanda. New Complementary Ontology Beyond World-Immanentism, Ethnocentric Reduction and Impositions,* Münster: Lit verlag, 2007.

Asouzu Innocent, *Ibuanyidanda (Complementary Reflection) and Some Basic Philosophical Problems in Africa Today,* Münster: Lit verlag, 2013.

Asouzu Innocent, *Ibuanyidanda (Special Edition),* Calabar: University of Calabar Press, 2013.

Bonachristus, *Principia Logica: A Most Complete Handbook of Logic(s),* Onitsha: Mid-Field Publishers, 1996.

Chimakonam, Jonathan O. "Why Can't There Be An African Logic?" *Integrative Humanism Journal,*1. 2. (2011), 141-152.

Chimakonam, Jonathan O. "The Criteria and Some Contemporary Methods in African Philosophy" Unpublished Paper.

Cook, Roy I. *A Dictionary of Philosophical Logic,* Edinburgh: Edinburgh University Press Ltd, 2009.

Descartes, Rene *A Discourse on Method, Meditations and Principles,* Trans. John Veritch, London: J. M Dent, 1994

Edet, Mesembe "Metaphysics, Contemporary African Philosophy and Ethnocentric Commitment." *Interractions in the History of Philosophy, (Conference Proceedings, PHILHIST'13), 2013*

Etuk, Udo, "The Possibility of African Logic". *The Third Way in African Philosophy: Essays in Honour of Kwasi Wiredu.* Olusegun Oladipo Ed. Ibadan: Hope Publication, 2002.

Enyimba, Maduka, "The Nature of Logic in African Philosophy". *Sophia: An African Journal of Philosophy,* 7.2. (2005), 51-58.

Ijiomah, Chris O. "Okolo's African Philosophy Revisited." *The Nigerian Journal of Theology,* 1.6, (1990), 94-105

Ijiomah, Chris O. *Contemporary Views about the Philosophy of Education,* Calabar: Uptrico Press, 1996.

Ijiomah, Chris O. "An Excavation of Logic in African World-View." African *Journal of Religion, Culture and Society,* 1.1 (2006), 29-39.

Iroegbu, Pantaleon, *Enwidomization and African Philosophy,* Owerri: International University Press, 1994

Jacquette, Dale "Introduction: Logic, Philosophy, and Philosophical Logic." *A Companion to Philosophical Logic*, D. Jacquette ed. Malden: Blackwell Publishing Ltd., 2006.

Jaja, Jones M. and Badey, Paul P. "Logic in African Philosophy: Examples from two Niger Delta Societies". *International Journal of Academic Research in Business and Social Sciences,* e.4. (2012), 95-102.

James, George G. M. *The Stolen Legacy: Greek,* New York: Philosophical Library, 1988.

Lacey, Alan *A Dictionary of Philosophy*, London: Routledge Press, 1996.

Makinde, Moses. A. *African Philosophy: The Demise of a Controversy*, (Selected Papers), Ile-Ife: Obafemi Awolowo University Press, 2010.

Momoh, Campbell. S. "The Logic Question in African Philosophy." *The Substance of African Philosophy,* Campbell S. Momoh Ed., Auchi: African Philosophy Projects Publications, 2000.

Momoh, Campbell. S. "Nature, Issues and Substance of African Philosophy" *The Substance of African Philosophy,* Campbell S. Momoh Ed., Auchi: African Philosophy Projects Publications, 2000.

Momoh, Campbell. S. "Elements of Formal Logic in Natural Language" *Philosophy for All Disciplines,* Jim I. Unah, Ed., Lagos: Promocomms Ltd, 2005.

Oguejiofor, Obi. *In Praise of African Philosophy*, (Nnamdi Azikiwe University Awka - Inaugural Lectures Series, No. 14), Enugu: Victojo Production Services, 2010.

Okolo, Chukwudum B. *African Philosophy: A Short Introduction* (Rev. ed.), Enugu: CECTA Nig. Limited, 1993.

Oladipo, Olusegun *The Idea of African Philosophy,* 3rd edn. Ibadan: Hope Publications, 2000.

Onyewueyi, Innocent I. *The African Origin of Greek Philosophy: An Exercise in* Afrocentrism, Nsukka: University of Nigeria Press, 1993.

Ozumba, Godfrey Okechukwu and Jonathan Okeke Chimakonam. *Njikoka Amaka: Further Discussion on the Philosophy of Integrative Humanism (A Contribution to African and Intercultural Philosophies).* Calabar: 3rd Logic Option, 2014.

Ozumba, Godfrey O. *Philosophy and Method of Integrative Humanism.* Calabar: Jochrisam, 2010.

Ruch, E. A. *The Ways of Knowing and Thinking*, Roma: University of Lesotho Press, 1977.

Sanguineti, Juan J. *Logic and Gnoseology,* Vatican: Urbaniana University Press, 1987.

Uduma, Oji. U. "Between Universalism and Cultural Identity: Revisiting the Motivation for an African Logic" A Paper Presented at the International Conference of the Council for Research in Values and Philosophy Washington DC, USA at University of Cape Coast, Cape Coast Ghana 3rd – 5th February, 2010

Uduma, Oji. U. "Can There Be African Logic" *From Footmarks to Landmarks on African Philosophy* Andrew F. Uduigwomen Ed. Lagos: Obaroh and Ogbinaka Publishers, 2009.

Uduma, Oji. U. *Introduction to Logic and the Fundamentals of Formal Reasoning*, Abakaliki: WillyRose & Appleseed Publishing Coy, 2008.

Uduma, Oji. U. *Modern Symbolic Logic*, Enugu: Pan-Afric Publishers, 2004.

Journal of Integrative Humanism – Ghana: Vol. 4 No. 1, October, 2014, ISSN: 2026-6286

DEVELOPING RURAL EDUCATION IN NIGERIA
BY
LILY N. OZUMBA

DEPARTMENT OF POLITICAL SCIENCE,
UNIVERSITY OF CALABAR

ABSTRACT

In this paper our attempt is dual. One is to identify factors that militate against the education of rural dwellers in Nigeria. Two, is to suggest ways of improving the educational standing of rural dwellers and to insist that the only sincere path to rural development in Nigeria is to educate the rural dwellers first so that they can get involved in the development of their areas of abode. We identified corruption, insensitivity, insincerity as some of the reasons why our rural communities have not been developed educationally. We have suggested as our theoretical framework the adoption of the structural theory which will involve an integrative approach as the only sincere way of bringing development through education to our rural dwellers. Government should systematically structure the educational policies so that all the facilities that are necessary for conducive learning environment are created in our rural communities. This is to reduce the refusal of teaching manpower to take up jobs in our rural communities.

Key-words: *Rural Development, Structural Theory and Rural Education.*

Introduction

Education is one aspect of Development that started after the 2nd world war in1945, when Nations began to think of how to develop, politically, socially and economically. This is not to say that prior to this time there was no education. Rather, it was this time that nations began to give serious thought to education as a vehicle for national and world cohesion.

Education is an instrument "per excellence" for effecting national development. It has witnessed active participation by non-governmental agencies, communities, and individuals as well as government intervention (National policy on education, 2004).Educational Planning in Nigeria dates back to 1942 when the colonial administration in Lagos drew up a Ten-year Education Plan for consideration by the colonial office in London. The Original plan was modified and in 1944 when Nigeria's first education plan took effect, Adesina and John, (1980). The first education plan was pervaded with deficiencies in that the policy was tactically designed to enhance the exploitative administration of the colonial masters. It was in the third national development plan (1975-80) that Universal Primary Education (UPE) was introduced in the country and the plan was geared toward increasing the literacy rate in the nation and thereby reducing the illiteracy rate which is seen among those who had no formal education. Arua and Duru (2011). It was to enable school leavers to be useful to themselves and the nation. Nyong (2005) pointed out that, the failure of UPE was a failure in planning and logistics, the Federal Ministry of Education as well as the State Ministries of Education were not informed when the programme was announced, implementation was a problem. The 6-3-3-4 was introduced which comprised 6 years of primary education, 3 years of junior secondary education, 3 years of secondary education and 4 years of higher education. It was introduced so that in the first 3 years of secondary education which includes prevocational subjects such as metal work, woodwork, technical drawing, etc. Those who want to seek employment at an early stage would already have had some training for it. But this also had some deficiencies because in Nigeria today very few secondary schools have adequate teachers and facilities for the teaching of science subjects which have impeded serious progress in technological research for economic growth and social well being of the people. The poor performance of 6-3-3-4 led to its modification and introduction of UBE. The fundamental principle of the UBE is that the Millennium Development Goals (MDGs) items two adopted by world nations in 2000 proposed that, by 2015, children of educatable age should have free, affordable and accessible education. The item is a response to the world conference of 'Education for All (EFA)" held in Jomitten, Thailand from 5th to 9th March 1990, which was the major trigger for the birth of basic education. Nigeria as a nation became encouraged to setup educational activities to achieve EFA goals at national level which asserted that everyone has the right to education. But all these had implementation problems.In 1999 during Obasanjo's regime, educational system was in a state of decay (FGN 2004). Teachers were poorly trained and motivated, high rate of illiteracy as a consequence of high dropout rates, poor infrastructural facilities in schools, etc. The introduction of the UBE came as a result of this long neglect of the education sector. The UBE is seen as a way of positively transforming the nation's basic education sub-sector (FGN 2004) and to meet the context of the global vision of EFA. Today, the UBE is here with us as it aims at equipping individuals with knowledge. This laudable programme is yet to be fully extended to the rural areas?

Policy on Rural Education

The Fourth National Development Plan 1981-85 proposed the integration approach to real development so as to evolve appropriate types of infrastructural facilities for the development of real potentials. Thus the plan declares the rural dwellers as constituting the 'centre –piece' of rural development strategy with the intention to realize new income opportunities through orienting rural communities to produce for markets. It was also the intention of the plan to rescue rural dwellers, through appropriate devices, from the ravages of diseases, malnutrition and ignorance. Furthermore, the plan declares that balanced development would receive a new boost and emphasis. … The policy of promoting a more rapid development of the rural areas through sustained efforts to raise productivity and provide basic human needs such as hygienic water supply, health facilities, access roads, electricity, education, etc., will continue. This strategy will help to provide a basis for more even geographic spread of physical development throughout the country. Isah (2007). Notwithstanding the acclamation contained in development plans, they have remained more problematic and insurmountable. Rural Nigeria cannot, for example, find good drinking water, basic health and educational services, etc.The failure to implement the development plans was not only because the government paid more attention to urban areas but also more importantly the political class to cushion theirvested interest squandered the petro-naira, which occurred during the phenomena of oil boom era.

Role of Local Government in Rural Development

Local government represents grassroots administration and by extension better placed to accelerate rural development. In rural countries like Nigeria where seventy-five percent(75%) of its population still resides in the rural areas, there is need for some kind of political arrangement which will allow local government to exert meaningful impact on the lives and aspiration of the masses which hitherto had been ''marginalized, ignored and abandoned in the scheme of things over the years''. Another area is that local government ensures political education at the grassroots and easy accountability of those elevated to public offices.Local governments are near the people so development programmes are often initiated, coordinated and most at times implemented by them. Local government is the third tier of government, the closest level of government to the down-trodden, poverty-ridden, disease infested and highly illiterate rural masses. Local governments were expected to be autonomous and more efficient in performing their functions. But we see that these expectations were hindered by the prevailing political beliefs or values of those in position of authority to influence the function, structure and compositions of local government system.Rural development often adopted by the military governments, is to set up centrally-controlled agents of grassroots development which are partially functional through the instrumentalities of local governments. They provide programme for the rural areas such as DEFRRI, Better life for rural women, Mamser, Family support Programme, etc. The question that mustbeasked is, how have we failed with these programmes.

Statistics on Rural Education in Nigeria

There is a growing awareness that research reports on educationaldevelopment in Nigeria has traditionally focused on studies carried out in the cities. Statistics available on educational development are mainly on enrolment in schools in the urban centers. It is easy to talk of the number of primary and secondary schools in towns, such statistics are hardly available about the educational development in therural areas. In contrast to the traditional approach of using the provided educational statistics about schools located in the urban centers in Nigeria to generalize for the urban and rural areas, whose figures are never really available, there has arisen therefore the need for a broader conceptualization of educational development in Nigeria to incorporate the much neglected rural areas, which also shows inequalities in educational development between the urban towns and the rural areas, which do not show up in national statistics and analysis. The implication of this neglect is that in educational advancement, urban centres will attract the establishment of schools because of the teeming population. The urban areas also began to attract teachers who liked to settle in towns to enjoy the social amenities that are provided in the urban areas. On the contrary, rural areas witnessed lack of establishment of schools. Where schools are available, teachers either resist or refuse transfers to those rural areas for lack of social amenities. Ezewu and Tahir (1997) analyze the effect of the lack of social amenities in an area to include inability to retain qualified and experienced teachers to man the few secondary and primary schools where they exist. It should also be noted, that this factor is responsible for lack of official records and statistics about educational development in the rural areas, particularly as school supervisors appointed by the state and other local government officials, appointed to monitor educational development are highly infrequent in the places they are assigned to monitor. In worse cases, government monitoring officials are non-existent in some rural areas. The effect of this is that there are no records about educational development in many rural areas in Nigeria.

Table showing level of disparity between urban and rural areas

[Note 1: The following Colunms in the table numberered 1-10 have the following entries:
1= Towns/Villages, 2 = Good Road, 3 = Electricity, 4 = Telephone Services, 5 = Health Facilities, 6 = Easy Means of Transportation, 7 = Good Water Supply, 8 = Recreation Centres, 9 = Good Houses, 10 = Schools, Educational Records & Statistics: Note 2: A = Available, NA = Not Available]

1	2	3	4	5	6	7	8	9	10
Calabar	A	A	A	A	A	A	A	A	A
Agbokin Waterfall	NA	NA	NA	NA	NA	NA	NA	NA	NA
Ekugha Tai	NA	NA	NA	NA	NA	NA	NA	NA	NA
Okosarah	NA	NA	NA	NA	NA	NA	NA	NA	NA
Yenegoa	A	A	A	A	A	A	A	A	A
Poloako	NA	NA	NA	NA	NA	NA	NA	NA	NA
Zarama	NA	NA	NA	NA	NA	NA	NA	NA	NA
Tombai	NA	NA	NA	NA	NA	NA	NA	NA	NA
Kano	A	A	A	A	A	A	A	A	A
Tsanyawa	A	NA	NA	NA	NA	NA	NA	NA	NA
Albasuo	A	NA	NA	NA	NA	NA	NA	NA	NA
Kunchi	A	NA	NA	NA	NA	NA	NA	NA	NA
Kaduna	A	A	A	A	A	A	A	A	A
Kujama	A	NA	NA	NA	NA	NA	NA	NA	NA
Kanfanchan	A	NA	NA	NA	NA	NA	NA	NA	A
Zonkwa	A	NA	NA	NA	NA	NA	NA	A	A
Benin City	A	A	A	A	A	A	A	A	A
Emunekhua	NA	NA	NA	NA	NA	NA	NA	NA	NA
Ugbomighan Erah	NA	NA	NA	NA	NA	NA	NA	NA	NA
Olinlin uzea	NA	NA	NA	NA	NA	NA	NA	NA	NA

Source: R.O.A. Aluede (2005) Field trips reports. Unpublished reports from field trips to Kano, Kaduna, Calabar, Yenegoa and Benin City.

From the table above, it is clear that towns that have social amenities communication facilities attract teachers and such places are often supervised. Educational statistics are easy to get concerning schools in urban centers. Rural areas like Agbokin water falls find it difficult to get boats; weather is also a strong factor in determining accessibility. All these affect education in rural areas with regards to educational data available to researchers. For this reasons ratios of illiteracy are frequently presented as averages; the actual distributionof illiteracy is either underestimated or unknown. This has serious consequences on the minorities or those in the rural areas because it often results in the inabilityof the nation-state to systematically plan for rural dwellerssolve the problems of those in rural areas, particularly as their levels of deprivation are not known. Furter (1980).

Also the education statistics gotten from UNICEF revealed that the rural areas are backward in education, see breakdown below.

Net Attendance Rate of Rural Primary School
Male = 61.9   female = 52.0

Net Attendance Rate of Urban Primary School
Male = 73.8   female = 70.6

Female/male ratio rural primary school   -   0.84
Female/male ratio urban primary school -   0.96

Net Attendance Rate of Rural Secondary School
Male = 31.7   Female = 25.9

Net Attendance Rate of Urban Secondary School
Male = 47.4   Female = 45.7

Female/male ratio rural secondary school   -   0.82
Female/male ratio urban secondary school -   0.96
(The above data was retrieved in January 2008 from UNESCO Institute for Statistics, Data Centre:
http://stats.uis.unesco.org/unesco/ReportFolders/ReportFolders.aspx).

The Mission of Education

The mission of education is to seek truth and propagate same undiluted, unembellished, and convincingly proven statistics that will be relevant for educational development at all times. If it is a fact, then there is no "Ifs" or 'buts". Nobody can truly claim to be educated who doctors the truth or manipulates facts in order to suit his or her whims and caprices. Fact is not like history said to be largely subjective, that can be doctored or manipulated. When you have arrived as a truly intellectually liberated person, is when you call facts and figures as you see them, no matter who it may concern, because truth is very exhilarating and bubbles like champagne wine. If you try to stand it on its head, it quickly reverts to its natural form- truth. And if you try to force it into your mind, it tastes sour. Truth is easier to manage, falsehood shifts like quicks and Nkwocha (2010).

Theoretical Framework
Structural Theory

This work adopts structural theory. According to Anam (2011) the prime focus of structural theory is on the transformation of major structures and the institutions in the society. They believe that if institutions and structures are transformed in line with modern or western democratic ideals, the society will develop, that is given attention to education and other institutional structures to meet the need of the society. To meet the target, educational institutions in the country should be directed in such a way that it will formulate education policy that favours the rural dwellers.

The underlining relevance of this theory to this study lies in their explanatory power; it describes how transformation of major institutions of the nation can be restructured to take care of rural areas. In the case of educational institutions, the strategy was to improve the literacy rate among the rural dwellers and this was pursued through educational policies such as vocational education, extension education, literacy programme, koranic education and non formal education.

Structural model has element of liberation, for example, the women liberation movement which is the restructuring of the family and the entire society especially the African society. It is the notion of this model that if structures like schools, health care centres, etc, are well equipped with good trained teachers, science textbooks, laboratory equipment, modern facilities and proper supervision just like it is obtain in Europe and North America, it would improve human capacity who would in turn bring about sustainable development. Structural model has widened our knowledge and understanding that training and empowering rural dwellers will bring about:

❖ Self-actualization
❖ Self reliance
❖ Fulfillment and satisfaction
❖ Independence - which would reduce poverty related problems.

From the view of the structural model, one realizes that education will strengthen as well as give women the ability for wealth creation and wealth distribution. It would help women to be educated and to be emancipated from the cultural belief that women's place is in the kitchen. With education, women would participate in production of goods and services as well as expose them to politics in the rural areas. This will also help to reduce unemployment; prostitution and poverty would be reduced as people would be working to help themselves.

Structural model has helped us discover that education is actually an effective tool in addressing rural povertyand rural urban migration. It focuses onrestructuring and transforming human capacity which will in turn effect a change in the rural area economically, politically, socially and culturally.

Developing Rural Education

Rural development is a deliberate effort mobilized to eradicate or reduce to the barest minimum social and economic ills that persist in diminishing the quality of life in the rural areas; it will include improvement of the social and economic conditions in rural places creating better job opportunities, increased family incomes and general attainment of well being.Bamidele (1990).

Rural development in Africa grew out of a substantial interest within the World Bank which sought ways of designing relevant projects that could be accomplished despite limited resources particularly of money and trained man power, and that would reach a large proportion of the low-income rural population. According to Uma Lele (1975) rural development is defined as improving living standard of the mass of the low-income population residing in rural areas and making the process of their development self-sustaining.Falade(1990) in Ozumba (1997) defines rural areas are those areas that lack the basic necessities oflife. They are areas that are characterized by poverty, relative deprivation, starvation and malnutrition, apathy, economic stagnation, poor quality of life, inadequate health facilities, poor educational opportunities, poor housing, inadequate representation, and in general do not evince a fair appropriation of their share of the nation's resources. These make them mostly pre-industrial and crudely agricultural. Development is an integrated, intricate, complex and multifaceted social phenomenon. It includes the economic, the political, environmental and the physiological. He also talked of development in terms of science and technology; it should be seen as overall growth and expansion in all the social dimensions of life. We should not talk of development in a partial sense. A humanistic approach will entail improvement of society's capacity to understand, manage and control its environment and not merely to exploit it.

Rural developers must therefore take into consideration the needs of the whole man- food, housing, good health, clean environment, basic education, etc.

Lack of Education to the Rural Areas

Education is a distinctive way in which the society inducts its young ones into full membership. So every modern society needs some educational policies to guide it in the process of such initiation (Okoroma, 2000).

Lack of education has kept some rural areasbackward and underdeveloped. They experience low per capital income, lower educational facilities, and few job opportunities and lack some essential infrastructures.

Education makes people feel special and want a better tomorrow, desire a sense of direction, and success. Unfortunately where there is no proper education things fall apart. For example, the issue of Boko-haram which has become a menace, creating insecurity in the minds of citizens as a result of high rate of bombing, shooting and killing of innocent citizens could be as a result of illiteracy. It is assumed that Boko-haramis a product of Almajiris in the North, people who roam the street without education, though some are educated but illiterate see Nyong's explanation below.These aremostly unskilled and unemployed youth wholack vision,unthoughtful youthswho could not discern between the truth and falsehood as Nkwoacha pointed out. The mission of education is to seek truth and propagate same undiluted, but when people are not properly educated, how can they know the truth talk less of defending the truth, whatever is told them as truth will be accepted by them. As Nyong (1997) puts it, education goes beyond literacy; someone may be literate but not educated. Education gives full commitment to the attainment of national objectives, so if one is educated he should know the truth and be committed to national objectives. It is illiteracy and general ignorance, coupled with the ingrained resistance to change that is proving a formidable obstacle to governance in Nigeria.

Importance of Education to the Rural Dwellers

A. Education Stimulate Local Initiative

When people are educated, they try to be involved in planning which will help to assess their own local needs, because they can now relate well as a result of education, but where they are not educated they cannot participate in rural development programmes that will enlighten them. Such programmes can be thwarted by subtle forms of paternalism. A case in Kenya, a city called Sook where special rural development programme was carried out in road construction. For the people, road construction meant more police coming in to arrest their cattle-raising activities, they were not involved in the planning, they knew nothing about it, so when tractors appeared to cut down trees, the people objected vigorously, until police was sent to guard the tractors, if the people were educated and were involved in the planning they would not have thwarted the project.

B. Education Eradicates Poverty.

Education as we say is crucial to the elimination of poverty; it provides skills and abilities which allow the poor to secure production and well-paying jobs. When people are educated and acquire jobs, they are not idle. Most of the problems we are having with the Niger delta boys and the Boko-haram who are kidnapping and terrorizing the country are because the Elite use these uneducated and jobless young boys to perpetuate evil. With monies diverted from the coffers of the federal or state governments are used to equipthese young men with latest weapons of destruction. Education increases the quality of life of the people; it is an instrument for excellence. It liberates people from poverty and ignorance Ukeje (1966). It is investment in people which pays bountiful dividend to the society. When that investment is not made or made inadequately, the society suffers loss. This is what Nigerian is suffering today from uneducated citizens who are now being bought to perpetuate evil in the society.

C. Education brings out the best in us

Ake (1988) said "education" is the process of becoming the best we can be, though the quality of education today is not at its best as expected.

49

Corruption has lowered down the standard of education, this is seen from the top when in 2005 during president Obasanjo's regime, Professor Fabian Osuji (the former Minister of Eduction) gave #55 million naira to some members of National Assembly before they could approve budget for the ministry of education Obasanjo (2005). All the facts available showed that the refusal to accede to such a bribery demand means doom for the education sector for the year. It is rather unfortunate that senators who are senior citizens unfortunately demanded an inducement before they would approve that Nigerian child should go to school. This is why the education sector in the country is in a deplorable state. Children now cheat at schools; parents register their children in special centers to pass examination. Teachersnow collect money from school children and allow them to cheat in examination; children are no more dependent on themselves in examination. Even in higher institutions, studentscannot perform well because of poor foundation from the onset, at post graduate level people cannot express themselves both in oral and written examinations.

D. Education Inculcate Societal Values in People.

Education for rural dwellers makes them to have societal values, obey rules and norms of the society. Education will help the rural dwellers to think of social change, and when you are thinking of social change it means you want good things to come to your society not desiring to destroy things. It will help them to adapt to changes, when people are not educated, it is difficult to adapt to change, rather they act in violent ways if one tries to bring about a change which they feel does not suit them.

Education makes them to think of ways to research into development than destruction. Education will help them to acquire prestigious jobs with higher certificates and anyone with a prestigious job cannot be idle and will not be interested in acts of violence. Education will help to mould their characters, and enable them to interact with other people regardless of their sect, tribe or religion and it will make them to have values for life. Education will help them develop or expose them to good ideas by way of enhancing their well being which will help them to contribute meaningfully to the society.

E. Education Provide Manpower Development to the Rural Dwellers

Education both formal and informal is the cornerstone of the human resources for technology. The world is changing with science and technology and anybody not educated is left out, this is why the rural dweller should be educated to expand their capacity to develop technology and make better use of technology which will help them exploit new information and adapt to changes. With the aid of technology they would be trained in some special areas such as technical, internet and other ICTs that will make them have access to information which will help them create innovation for change and transformation. When they are developed and a lot is invested into them, it will reduce poverty. Development provides skill and ability which will lead to competition and consequently lead to the development of the economy. Education makes them to adapt to technology to fit into any conditions, whether in agriculture, carpentry, etc. Technology is necessary, for instance the neglect of technology for food crops not only affects rural welfare; it also arrests rural growth. Education improves the content of training and makes it more practical. Training programmes can, of course improve specific rural development programmes.

F. Education Bridge Information Gap in Rural Areas

According to Bassey Anam (2011) access to information is a key resource for local people in maintaining active and independent lives. It helps them to know government programmes, their roles and sources of support and benefit to be derived from such programs. The challenges of rural development cannot be achieved without the development of an effective information base in the rural communities. Information transmitted most of the times gets distorted, but if the rural dwellers, understand what is being told them without a third party, it is better. Information is needed in the areas of Agriculture that is, learning best forms of farming practices such as, planting, treating seed, soil conservation, etc. Information is needed about where they can obtain loans to build houses or improve on their farming. Information is required on issues of welfare, how to take care of themselves while working, even on employment opportunities or skill acquisition. They need to know how they can exercise their political right, and how to report any crime against them.

Ways of Educating the Rural Dwellers

The following can be organized for their education:

Extension Education: where they are trained to upgrade their competence or skills in specific areas such as agriculture, health, home management, small scale industries, etc.

Adult Education: where they are taught how to read and write, this can be concluded in mutually agreed locations including open spaces under trees, using Church buildings or in school buildings mostly in the evenings when school children must have gone home. There is need to be simple while educating the rural dwellers, but most of the times, the teachers use borrowed phrases and jargons and terminologies which are foreign to the people and thus succeed in beclouding the issues and thereby confusing them.

Women Education

There is need to established the women extension unit, which may be centered largely on welfare, such as hygiene, nutrition, meal preparation, and gardening. Education bestows on women a disposition for a lifelong acquisition of knowledge, values, attitudes, competence and skills.

Vocational Skills

Several efforts can be made to provide vocational training to adults. Example, blacksmithing which can make them to make and repair farming/other implements that will help them become multi-cultivators.

General training for rural needs

These can promote manufacturing skills in the rural sector, there could be training in general agriculture, nutrition, since the main thrust of rural training has been on the activities related to agriculture and social services.

Rural /Urban Drift

With the help of education rural migration drift will reduce, when the rural areas are not developed withany social amenities, people drift to the urban areas which also pose problem to the urban areas. More so the country will suffer hunger as most farmers will drift to the urban centers, there will also be infrastructural problem in the urban areas as a result of the drift to the urban areas.Government should provide social amenities that are available in the town or urban centers in the rural areas. This will make the urban centers less attractive.

Recommendation

You can alleviate some one's poor life but still keep him or her poor; to help the person improved economically is to educate the person to be self reliant. If the pivot on which development hangs is the people- who are defined in the UNDP's Human Development Report 1990 as ' the real wealth of a nation- the question then is; what will motivate an individual to want to give his/her best to achieve the highest level of productivity possible. Education, skill, technology are important in this regardAsante (1991). For rural development to be viable in the long run, rural institution is necessary, it is to sensitize rural people and thus increase the receptivity and ability of rural people to respond to development programmes which encourage local initiative.

Our Leaders should invest money into the rural areas to encourage teachers and supervisors.Government should build modern schools in rural areas and provide staff quarters with communication net work, electricity, good water to attract teacher to the rural areas. There should be some form of inducements granted by the government to staff posted to the rural areas in Nigeria. Government could run a different pay structure for teachers and other staffs in the rural areas.

The East Asian miracle, the fantastic success of the East Asian countries particularly China and Taiwan has been attributed to their governments' investment of enormous resources to the development of the rural areas.Nigeria should learn from this.

Literacy has been one of the major constraints in introducing a wide range of programmes to rural people; illiteracy is a constraint in broadening participation in rural development programmes and poses a serious risk that the educated will exploit the illiterate. A case in Cameroon, Zapi and Sodenkan town showed that because of lack of education they are being exploited by the educated ones especially at trading, and so it was pointed out that the only way to prevent malfeasance at the marketing level is to give the pioneers the training they need in order to be able to check the weighing of produce and understandUma Lele.(1975).With education they will not be cheated.

When rural dwellers are trained they will remain there and produce to boost the income of the nation. In 1962, USAID supported programme for promoting small industries in northern Nigeria, like Industrial Development Center (IDC) at Zaria, the scope of the programme was blacksmithing,auto repairing to leather working and carpentry.Unfortunately, upto 1970 these workshops did not produce training in how to operate the new equipment brought in under the programme, so it did not work out.

No great improvements in the lot of mankind are possible, until a great change takes place in the fundamental constitution of their modes of thought. Stuart(1991). Development should not be undertaken on behalf of the people, but by them; it should be the organic outcome of society's value system, its perceptions, its concerns and its endeavors. As such, to achieve and sustain development, it is necessary to ensure the education and training of the people so they can participate fully and effectively in the development process Adedeji (1991).

He also pointed out that development refers to human beings, to every man and woman, to the whole man and the woman. For development of human, experience is synonymous with the fulfillment of individual mental, emotional and physical well being, and not just the growth of things, which are merely means which needs education. In other words, development is not merely a transformation of the structures and material attribute of a society. Authentic, self-reliant processes of development inevitably result in the transformation of the people who bring about the change- their culture, attitude to work, their saving and investment habit, their concept and skills and their social system. Genuine self-reliant development of any economy results in the process of transformation of the people and these cannot come without education.

Conclusion

Efforts have been made to develop education in Nigeria since independence in 1960. Various policies in the interest of education have been formulated, some of which have been presented in this paper. Unfortunately, these efforts have not produced the desired effect. In the final analysis, Nigeria's development failures have sprung from the lack of success in achieving an effective model of governance. At the head of this problem has been instability generated by the rivalry for control of the huge resources accruing to the state from the oil industry, and the use of political power to milk the state for personal gain rather than promote economic and social development. The issue of corruption in education has already been mentioned in this work. The cankerworms of corruption and gross mismanagement of resources have been blamed for the deplorable state of the country's educational system.

Government talks of poverty reduction and economic empowerment, that is, government is working on halving poverty by the year 2015, in line with the MDGs and recognizes that improvements in economic growth have to be accompanied by policies that improve opportunities for employment, income generation and access to resources among the poorest groups in society, and such services scheme include programmes on qualitative education.

Finally, good governance is fundamental to national development and that sustainable development cannot thrive on its own without sustainable democracy. A good governance adopt good framework that support human development, monitors it, ensure effective and efficient implementation of whatever policy has been adopted. Money without education is insufficient.

References

Arua, J. and Duru, E.J.C. (2011). *Development Administration in Nigeria Issues Principles and Strategies*, Aba: Global Prints Ltd.

Adesina, S. and Johnson T, (1980). *Cost Benefit Analysis of Education in Nigeria,* Lagos, Nigeria: Lagos University Press Monograph series.

Anam, Bassey (2011), *Understanding Rural Development: Concept, Theories and Strategies* Calabar: Kings view Publishing House

Asante, S.K.B. (1991) *African Development: Adebayo Adedeji's Alternative Strategies.* Ibadan: Spectrum Books.

Aluede, R. O. A. (2005). Field Trips Report. Unpublished Reports from Field Trips to Kano, Kaduna, Calabar, Benin City.

Adebayo, Adedeji in Asante, S.K.B. (1991) *African Development: Alternative Strategies.* Ibadan: Spectrum Books.

Adighije, C. (2005), Saturday Sun News paper, 9 April, p.5.

Alan B. Mountjoy (1966) *Industrialization and Underdevelopment Countries.* Chicago: Aldine Publishing Company

Ake, C. (1988). "Quality Education in a Dwindling Economy", Lecture Delivered on the occasion of the 11[th]Convocation Ceremony of the Rivers State College of Education, Port Harcourt.

Barnes C. (1972) "Kapauguria SRDP. An Evaluation" in *An Overall 1972 Evaluation of the Special Rural Development Programme,* Nairobi Institute for Development Studies. Paper No. 8.

Bamidele, S. A(1990in Ozumba 1997) *Nigeria Government and Politics.* Aba. AAU Industries.

Burnhan Peter & Charles Jones, (2003) *The Concise Oxford Dictionary of Politics,* Oxford: Oxford University Press.

Journal of Integrative Humanism – Ghana: Vol. 4 No. 1, October, 2014, ISSN: 2026-6286

Ezewu, E. E. and Gidado Tahir, (1997), *Ecology and Education in Nigeria,* Onitsha: Tabansi Publishers Ltd.

Ejiogu, B. (2005) Daily Sun Newspaper, Monday, 11 April, p.10.

Falade (1990) in Ozumba 1997*Nigerian Government and Politics* 1997. Aba: A.A.U. Publishers.

Furter, P. (1980) (2005), Educational Development in Nigeria:How Far can it be managed to incorporate the Rural Areas? Edo State. Field Trip Report.

Isah,M.A.(2007 in Anam 2011),*Understanding RuralDevelopment: Concept, Theories and Strategies* Calabar: Kings view Publishing House

Mill, John Stuart. (1991) in *African Development*: Adebayo Adedeji'sAlternative Strategies. Ibadan. Nigeria.Spectrum Books.

Nyong, M.O.(2001) *Public Policy, Public Sector Economics andManagement in Nigeria.*Calabar. A &A. Communication.

Nkwocha O.N (2010) Afulezi ' '*Igbo information, Art and Life in Africa'*'uafuleze@ hotmail.co.

News watch Nigeria weekly magazine, August, 1st 2011 Boko-haram Killings, the shocking details. Pp. 14-20.

Obasanjo, O. (2005) Educational Policies and Problems ofImplementation in Nigeria. Austrian Journal of Adult Learning. Volume.46, November 2, July 2006.

Osuji, F. (2005) Australian Journal of Adult Learning. Volume 56,July 2006.

Okoroma, N.S. (2006) Educational Policies and Problems ofImplementation in Nigeria. Rivers State University of Scienceand Technology Nigeria.

Ollawa (1981) in Duru and Arua (2010) *Development Administration In Nigeria Issues principles and Strategies.* Aba:Gheedal Global Print

Ukeje, C. (2006) *The challenges Affecting the Implementation of the Universal Basic Education* (UBE) in Nigeria.Delta. Volume 46,

UNESCOInstituteforStatistics,Datacentre,http://stats,uis,unesco.org/unesco/ReportFolders/ReportFolders.aspx, January 2008.

Uma, Lele .(1975) *The Design of Rural development.* London: John Hopkins University Press.

Journal of Integrative Humanism – Ghana: Vol. 4 No. 1, October, 2014, ISSN: 2026-6286

EXPLORING THE POTENTIALS OF COMMUNITY THEATRE AS A TOOL FOR SOCIAL CHANGE: THE PARTICIPATORY COMMUNICATION METHOD

BY

*ADIE EDWARD U., ** OKORO, LILIAN A. & ***ORIM, EUGENIA G.
DEPARTMENT OF THEATRE AND MEDIA STUDIES,
UNIVERSITY OF CALABAR, CALABAR-NIGERIA
*eddytorial@yahoo.com, **paciafrica@yahoo.com, ***g-bakery@yahoo.com

ABSTRACT

It is observed that most development modalities employed over the years for achieving community development in Africa have not leaved up to expectation in terms of involving the majority of people in the quest for national transformation and development; rather, these modalities tend to complicate the very problems they are set out to solve. The situation is mostly like this because the adopted development strategies have not taken adequate cognizance of the essence of effective communication methods and the importance of people's perspectives and peculiarities in these processes. Mostly, the so-called outsiders and experts in development matters who are physically and socially separated from the people think for them and about their development. This situation is inimical to genuine and sustainable development. It is important therefore to note that development can only be meaningful and sustainable when it is people generated; involving people's real needs and their participation in the process of achieving them. It is at this point therefore that community theatre can come handy as it has the potentials to bring people together to discuss issues that disempower them and participatorily proffer solutions to the negatives. Community theatre can be explored to work with rural and urban people; mostly the rural dwellers who are mostly disempowered. In view of this therefore, this paper posits that community theatre is a method of participatory communication towards achieving social change.

Key-words: *Community Theatre, Social Change, Participatory Communication, Culture*

Introduction

It is important to define participatory communication (PC) and its nuances before an attempt to establish its areas of convergence with Community Theatre. In this light therefore, Bessette (2005) posits that participatory communication is a process by which people become leading actors in their own development. It empowers people to move from being objects or recipients of development interventions to being the initiators of their own development. It is a communication method that puts the people in the driver's seat throughout the development process. This approach, according to Bessette, is gradually gaining more significance in the development world and is based on dialogue in which listening is as important as talking and one is not complete without the other. The importance of this two way communication model is to entrench trust, love and consensus in order to analyze one another's perceptions, ideas, opinions, available opportunities and potentials in solving observed problems and bringing about desired change.

According to Garland (2004)

> *Participatory communication is a planned activity, based on the one hand, on participatory processes, on media and interpersonal communication, which facilitates dialogue among different stakeholders, around common development problems or goals, with the objective of developing and implementing a set of activities to contribute to its solution or its realization and which supports and accompanies this initiative.*

The stakeholders Garland talked about above are the community members, local authorities, NGOs, Community Based Organizations(CBOs) and other institutions working at the community level as well as policy-makers who are involved in a given development initiative. This kind of communication means moving from a focus of informing and persuading people to facilitating interface and exchanges between stakeholders in order to address a common problem that could result in social and attitude change. Among others, participatory communication articulates the following characteristic features:

i) Participation is the watchword
ii) It anchored on dialogue
iii) It adopts bottom-top communication system
iv) It is cultural sensitive
v) It is directed at attaining empowerment, capacity building and sustainable development of local people.

The enlisted features represent very few of the numerous tenets of participatory communication. It is interesting to point out that, by definition and intention of Community Theatre earlier discussed, Community Theatre subscribes to the tenets or Participatory Communication and clearly dovetails into its core assumptions. Its ability to practicalise participatory communication is attributable to a number of functions as articulated by Iyorwuese et al (2011).

i) First, community theatre is a collective activity stressing creative communal participation instead of a few people (elites) who exercise their power by imposing their idiosyncrasies on the people.

ii) Secondly, community theatre uses the language and the cultural forms of the people thus encouraging indigenous creative expressions that were killed progressively over the years by missionary, colonialism and elite negligence.

iii) Thirdly, community theatre as a theatrical representation is useful in framing or modifying a piece of problem or reality. Through the medium of fiction with characters and situation, it holds up problems of local relevance for people to contemplate. In so doing, it helps to take a fresh look at their situations with a view to changing it.

iv) An important dimension of community theatre is discussion and evaluation, a process of dialogue which helps in further clarifying the problems dramatized before the final and most important step which is action for social change.

Methodology of Community Theatre

As a matter of fact, the methodological approach of community theatre is woven around carrying out investigative research within a given community, analyzing the information to gain a deeper understanding of the contradictions, building up a scenario within which to illustrate the issues, putting up a performance followed by a discussion and possible mobilization for action. This methodology seems to be the approach best suited for the kind of workshop and community theatre projects in Africa in recent years. We shall briefly review some of the basic elements of Ross kidd and Byram standard methodology as captured by some theatre scholars especially Lawal (2010), Abah (1997), Okwori (1994) as follows:

* Training the participants
* Community research and data collection
* Data analysis
* Scenario building

* Rehearsal/performance
* Post performance analysis
* Follow-through

It is important to note here that the methodology as put above is not given or constant. It could be adjusted as appropriate to match any Community Theatre field work peculiarity.

The Participants Training

The first step in this methodology comprises training the resource catalyst group who will be working with the target community.The essence is to teach the rudiments of organization for social mobilization and transformation. Lawal (2010) stresses the fact that training is also meant to enhance the pedagogical technique of instructing adults through a dialogue process of give and take.

Researching Community

This is a process of collecting information from the villagers themselves on what they regard as their problems. Various approaches on information gathering can be adopted but it is the situation on the ground that can determine which research approach is most appropriate some of the approaches include the Home Stead Method, the Migrant Method, the Interview Method, Flooding method, Hierarchical method and so on. Whichever approach is used, efforts must be made to draw out opinions on the problems from every available stratum of the community. In this regard, it will be necessary to obtain information on the community's problem from members of all social groups, all age-groups, and all economic and religious groupings. Such a wide spectrum of opinions will offer a wider perspective to the problem of the village or community.

Data Analysis

Once quality information is gathered, it is prioritized and analyzed by all participants. This according to Okwori (1994) is to ensure collective reflection on the problems of the community. It enables the participants to critically understand the problem and the strategies for solving them by overcoming fears and superstitions. This step is useful to get to the root cause of the problems, link them to micro and macro socio-economic and political determinants, prioritize issues, identify the ones that are subject to solute at the local level and through the drama process, discuss possibilities for channeling the ones that are beyond the community's capacity to appropriate quarters. In doing this, representative opinions of youths, women, men, children are sought.

Scenario building

After the analysis of the problems, the group then decides which of the problems can make good drama and how these problems can be tied into one story. Sometimes, the villagers themselves may be asked to act out a principal problem as it occurs in the village so as to give a more graphic view situation. In developing a scenario, a lot of creative thinking must be involved in trying to tie the various problems together otherwise the drama may appear as a series of plays brought together without any logic.

Performance

Through the process described above, a finished play is arrived at. A day and time are fixed for the final performance and the villages are left to do the publicity themselves, using the indigenous systems of disseminating information. The whole village gathers at the appointed time and place and watches the finished drama. After performance comes evaluation. This is a critical evaluation of the drama and its significance to the life of the villagers.

Community Theatre and Social Change

It is very necessary to define social change before we go further to examine how the community theatre fosters it. Rogers (1989) sees social change as the process by which alternations occur in the structure and function of a social system. The social system in this definition may be a social group, a community, a city, a region or a nation. Any change that occurs either in ideas, norms, values, roles and social habits of a people or in the composition or organization of society can be referred to as social change.

In the same way, Nair and White (1993) define social change as the process of raising the quality of life for the poor through communication and information processes which alter attitudes and behaviors of rural society and this enables their participation in development. To Burkey (1993):

> *Social change is a process of transformation in which people increase their awareness of their knowledge to analyze their needs; decide on solutions, organize themselves for cooperative efforts; and mobilizing their own human, financial and natural resources to improve, establish and maintain their*

own social service and institutions within the context of their own cultural political system.

One basic feature in the life of all living things is change. When it takes place in the lives of interacting human beings, it is termed social change; when it is viewed within the communal setting, it is termed communal social change the fact is that changes take place in the rural sub-urban and urban areas. Change could be in all attributes of a societal unit. It could be introduced from internal or external sources to the society or both. Having said this, we may now interrogate the place of community theatre in social change. Several factors come to mind in the process of discussing community theatre as a tool of social change. We shall only consider a few of these factors and constitute them as our canons or anchor to explicate the place of community theatre in communal social change. Such factors include:

1.   Participation in development process
2.   Cultural projection
3.   Education for employment

Participation for Social Change

As earlier indicated, participation is the stock-in-trade of community theatre. Community theatre is a participatory theatre which everyone that aspires for change must take part in. This is because, one cannot effect change without being involved in the larger process of change. The ease with which community theatre is accepted as a development tool in the developing countries, particularly in Nigeria, is due to its horizontal communicative ability and its participatory approach to issues.

Based on the above, Okwori in Abah (1997) posits that community theatre has come to be accepted as the people's theatre. This is because it deals with the issues and problems of the people. It uses their cultural forms, challenges them to become engaged in changing their realities and leaves the process of creativity and sharing in their own hands

Contributing to this discussion, Abah (1990) notes that:

Community theatre is not a professional affair and therefore, does not require professional attitudes to harness it. What it requires is the collective aspiration and decision of people wanting to use the theatre to develop their environment... community theatre entails the use of communal participation from problem identification and research to staging.

Reinforcing the above quotation, Abah (1990) further argues that the ethics of participatory community theatre is therefore participation and change. It is a process of learning which involves both the theatre and community. It is this aesthetics, which allows for an ever-deepening analysis based on active participation, that is anti-theatrical to the elites concept and approach. Obadiegwu (1994) adds that the community theatre is geared towards demystifying the popular idea held by elites that only professionals in the area of theatre can use theatre for the benefit of the society. This demythologization is contained in the ethics and aesthetics for integrated human development, which could be summed up in the injunction of a Chinese community organizer:

> *"Go to the people*
> *Live among the people*
> *Learn from the people*
> *Work with the people*
> *Start with what they know*
> *Build on what the people have*
> *Learn by doing.*

The above postulation has been the participatory strategy adopted by community theatre workers throughout the world. Most elite especially from the ivory tower are engaged in this arduous task of organizing rural urban people in the use of the art of the community theatre to drive change.

The community theatre as a participatory communication technique has undoubtedly been viable method for generating community involvement, in discussing communal issues and seeking joint method for action. According to Eyoh (1987), the implications of using community theatre as a participatory tool for social change are quite enormous. Undoubtedly, the participatory process provides a forum for collective interrogation towards a communal search for a better life; it creates a dialectical context within which the past can be used to inform the present and shape the future; it provides humanity with the possibilities to set its own agendas and set their realization, it gives a better understanding of their situations; it allows them a format/platform to hold discussions, it incites the people to mobilize themselves for action and creates an organizational structure for further action within the community it helps to catalyze the articulation of problems, the discussion of the basic contradictions within the community and helps strongly to create a reflection of their aspirations and total psyche. The final result of this communal participatory effort is to create a people's theatre with the view to instigating the process of social change.

Community theatre generates participation and participation in turn, produces self expression in the development process. Self expression increases confidence and self-knowledge, self-expression increases opportunity for creativity and this creativity transforms the community stakeholders from passive observers to active engagement in change-oriented dramatic action. Through community theatre, the community stakeholders are encouraged to development critical ways of looking at problems and situations so that can learn to work out new strategies for social change. This is achieved through dramatization, role analysis, play criticism and evaluation. To this end, community theatre serves to bring people together for solidarity, for celebration of important victories, for building confidence in popular power, for deepening the community's discussion and understanding of the major issues, for posing fun, stirring emotion and producing concrete possibilities for driving social change through participatory approaches.

Social Change via Cultural Projection

The very dynamic relationship between culture of a people and their development cannot be overemphasized, Culture is what makes a people; community theatre as a process and practice of Development Communication is often associated with and realized through the deploying of community cultural values, ideas, aspirations and their nuances of expression. Community theatre deploys the cultural practices of the people with a view to stimulating social change. Culture as a term, has a very wide range of both usage and application. In the context of social change, however, the concept of cultural projection requires not only the promotion of community cultural values necessary for community as a given entity including both its materials and non-material aspects. In view of the above, it is very imperative for the development catalysts using participatory community theatre to begin by studying the people's culture and its relevance to social change. To deny the relevance of the people's culture in their overall development process is to cripple change initiate fast. The native or communal people are quite inventive, creative and have imaginative range of expression. This mode of expression is part of their culture. Cabral (1977) notes that:

> It is generally in culture that the seed of protest, leading to the emergence and development of the liberation movement is found: they need to retrieve their past culture and use it to

> *develop their situation, instead of imposing alien culture that perpetuates dependency in them. This retrieved of culture is the need the development facilitator must start from. This may pose the problem of how to communicate with the people using their basic language and idiom.*

In view of the above quotation, most community theatre practitioners who are strongly in pursuit of change goals have cultivated the consciousness of putting the community cultures on pedestals knowing fully well that culture can either enhance or inhibit development processes. They therefore, encourage the communal people to document, store and disseminate in their own language their ongoing experience for progressive advancement of their collective knowledge based on their collective efforts. They are also encouraged to use their cultural traditions of storytelling, drama, poetry to document and disseminate their knowledge, and to take their experience to other groups and villages. Community theatre, in pursuit of social change also provides alterative cultural mode of expression. It attempts to return the theatre to its communal traditional function as an instrument of expression recognizing culture as the very life blood of truthful communication. It is only through cultural method that participatory community theatre becomes very effective means of advancing development efforts of the people. Any idea of community development that does not take into consideration elements within such environment would be inadequate.

The overall goal of the community theatre can be enhanced with a requite dose of cultural elements with which the community does not only readily identify with, but which they can appropriate in the task of self representation as the ultimate goal of community theatre.

This is true of the community theatre if it is to remain a people's oriented medium for self-expression and development. The involvement of cultural framework in the process of the community theatre is to the extent that it facilities far easier and amenable means of exploring, tapping and deploying the community's nuances, values, ideas and general communicative expression towards social change.

In view of the above, Forum Theatre (2001) believes that, using the cultural tool and framework, community theatre practice can help to stimulate social change in following ways:

1.   By encouraging lucid learning which offers people possibility communicate easier, to see things in a new and liberate for

stereotypes: to promote the equally among communal stakeholders and offer the possibility to create a vision.

2. By positively influencing the associative local capacities and the capacity to analyse local problem.

3. By creating a stimulant and flexible working environment, so that new behaviours, new kind of relationships can be exercised and learned in the community in order to consider the needs of the oppressed/powerless members of the community.

However, Buratai in Okwori (2004) believes that if community theatre must drive change from cultural perspective, the following rubric must be taken into cognizance:

a) The need to study, understand and deploy the various cultural patterns and genera social nuances of the community in which the community theatre project is located.

b) The need to delineate the elements of (a) above in terms of their cultural and communicate potentials in order to select those i.e. songs, music, dances, folktales etc which can be adapted to the strategy of the community theatre and the same time meets the needs of community cultural promotion and identity.

c) The need to look out for community cultural, behavioural and attitudinal perceptions and disposition, within the wider context of socio-cultural and customary biases as are likely to be encountered and which may turn out to be inhibitive to the task of the community theatre in a development project.

d) The need to identify and cultivate existing cultural groups in the community with the values and ideals of the community theatre in order to transform it from an alien and abstract concept into a tangible and visible feature of community life, to be appropriated and deployed by the community.

e) The need to be as vigilant and alert towards possible areas of cultural differences that may result in friction and therefore obliterate the goals of the community theatre.

Education for Social Change

In recent years, African art especially the community theatre is reaffirming its functionality. The role of community theatre in social education has been acknowledged worldwide. Mbachaga (2011) observes that Social education programmes particularly those geared towards development generally, have sprung up in many parts of the 3rd world: Brazil, Mexico, Kenya, Ghana, Zambia, Tanzania, Cameroon, Nigeria etc. Organisers of these programmes attest to the validation of the performing culture of the people. It has been observed that popular performing culture should not be seen as mere performances of folksongs and dances but event that have far reach implications in the daily life of the people."

The above quotation implies that the process of using theatre to mobilize and motivate participation as well as educate rural community is a task that entails using community theatre to enhance social change. He further argues that the cognitive value of community theatre as an art rests on its capacity to stir up a thought that propels the target audience to development an approach that confirms to the situation to address issues raised in the theatre. In this sense, the theatre activist automatically becomes a popular educator. Contributing to this issue, Eyo(1986) pontificates that "theatre (community theatre) in particular is being used in community education to conscientize and mobilize marginalized group of society who have been deprived access to the more conventional forms of media".

With the influence of Freire (1972) and Boal (1974), many theatre practitioners and adult educators have sought to rediscover community theatre's potential as a tool for mobilization. Community theatre as used in Africa, has the potential to stimulate community thinking, develop self-confidence, interactive expression, awareness and organization strengths of popular groups, communities and organizations (Ross Kidd, 1982). In the same vein, Bryan et al (1981) add that community theatre educates the populace in its pursuit of social change by building on the skills the people have. As an educational strategy, it combines the entertainment values of the performing arts with the capacity to highlight issues in relation to social change. Through dramatization, people's attention can be focused on problems in a way that challenges their perception of their situation. They are encouraged to take a fresh look at the situation and work out new solution. They are respect, community theatre is used as a two way communication process for education; it serves as a catalyst for involving people in discussion and action on their problems rather than merely accepting their lot or waiting for extern solutions.

Furthermore, in using community theatre for education that will propel social change, Bryan et al (2011) argued that it can stimulate critical analysis, organization and reinforcing growth of identity and self confidence. The codification of experiences is particular to the given community and emanates from their own experiences. Community theatre, according to them can intervene in several areas of community education and has proven itself to be more effective than many other forms of communication. These areas include non-formal education, health education campaigns, agricultural extension campaigns, community development projects intended to motivate self-help and mass sensitization campaign etc. Community theatre seems most viable in self- mobilization, education and collective action of people.

Conclusion

Community theatre, as elucidated above, is a theatre of the people, by the people and for the people which uses the expressive medium of the environment, and which treats the actual problem of the environment, highlighting them and opening discussion on them so that solutions to these problems can be worked out. It is a participatory theatre that acknowledges the creative and collective potentials of people towards solving problems for the common good of all in a Community.

References

Alachi, J. A. (2008) *Theatre for Development in the Benue Valley Makurdi:* Bookmakers Publisher.

Abah, O. S. (1997) *Performing Life: Case Studies in the Practice of Theatre for Development* Zaria: Bright Printing Press.

Abah, O. S.(1990) Participatory Theatre: Issues and Cases in Hagher (ed) the Practice of Community Theatre in Nigeria Jos.

Bryan, Martin, Moitse, Frances and Boeren Ad. Report of the Workshop on theatre for integrated Development, Mbabane, Department of Extra Mutal Studies, University of Swaziland, 1981.

Burkey, S. (1993). *People First: A Guide to Self-Reliant, Participatory Rural Development.* London Zedbooks Ltd.

Edeam, D. (1993). *Role of Development Journalism in Nigeria's Development.* Gazette.

Journal of Integrative Humanism – Ghana: Vol. 4 No. 1, October, 2014, ISSN: 2026-6286

Eyoh, H. N. (1987). *Theatre and Community Education: the Africa Experience* African council on communication education.

Garland, S. (2004). The researcher of Development Practitioner as Communication Actor,. IDRC Limitations of Development Communication Htm. 95/6/2005:6:31.

Kidd, R. (1990). " People Theatre, Conscientization and Struggle" in Media Development London:vol. 27 No.3.

Lawal, H. O. (2010). *Fundamentals of theatre Arts*. Glory land publishing company.

Machaga, J. D. (2011). *Theatre forDevelopment: an Approach to Safer Sex education: A guide for Teenagers Parents and practitioner:* Markurdi: bookmakers publishing.

Nair, K. And White, S. (1987). "The Development Communciation Process: A reconceptualization Delhi SAGE Publication Ltd.

Okwori, J. Z. (2004) (ed) *Community Theatre: An introductory Course* Book Zaria. Tamaza Publishing Company.

Okwori, J. Z. (1994). Empowering the Disempowered: using Popular Theatre fir Rural Transformation in Nigeria in Abah.

Rose, Kidd "Plays for Farmers: popular drama workshops in Northern Nigeria" Theatre International, 6(2): 1982, pp. 25-44.

Umar-Buratai, M. I. Community Theatre and Cultural Projection in Okwori J. Z. (2004) (ed) *Community Theatre: an Introductory* Course Book. Zaria: Tamaza Publishing Company.

DEVELOPMENT OF NIGERIAN ADVERTISING AND MEDIA EXCHANGE: A POST MODERN PERSPECTIVE

BY
*APEH, COLUMBA & **LAWRENCE EKWOK
DEPARTMENT OF THEATRE AND MEDIA STUDIES
UNIVERSITY OF CALABAR, CALABAR
*apehcolumba@gmail.com, **merlaw2002@yahoo.com

ABSTRACT

The main points of this research paper are to discuss advertising and media exchange in Nigeria from the very beginnings to the present day and future prospects. The earliest codified record of activities that could be classified as advertising dated as far back as the existence of man, although its identification as a business factor originated from the Roman imperial days when hired heralds were used to proclaim, often, state paid announcements. The urge to promote one's goods and services dates to the primordial age of man, and only the techniques, tactics and the modes have continued to improve with technology and modernization. Nigeria has witnessed massive commercialization, new merchandising centres developed in almost all parts and corners of the entire nation through the rapid improvement and development of the media industry.

Key-words: *Development, advertising, Post Modern, Media Exchange, Nigerian advertising*

Introduction

One of the banes of advertising in Nigeria is the absence of, or the existence of superficial education in the principles behind the practice of advertising. This had an offshoot from the early days of the profession, when the practitioners went bang into action from their various callings-largely the mass media and public relations. According to APCON (*Code of Advertising Practice*), defines advertising as the,

> ...form of communication through media about products services or ideas paid for by an identified sponsor... or as creative commercial communication, one needs to attempt to explain its significance. Understanding advertising is perhaps better done

from viewing its application-what it does, rather than
what it is, and how it does it (2).

Through the stages of human existence, as newer lifestyles evolved,
so has man's quest for self-sustenance and independence. With the trend trade-
first by barter earlier, and later media exchange, like the talent through time to
the cowries, the Manilla and today's currency (Naira in Nigeria). Commerce
brought competition and competition brought advertising (Bel-Molokwu 16).
In an attempt to trace the beginnings of advertising and media exchange, Pride
and Ferrel hold that,

> Modern advertising may be traced to the middle ages
> when, in the boom of organized commerce,
> enterprising dealers used signs to attract attention to
> their merchandise, often sold in demarcated areas in
> each town (98).

The arts, most especially the dramatic literature, no doubt, from the
beginning had a salient role to play in advertising and media exchange, and
have retained this role. The signs of old were often pictorial and with time,
words began to make their inroad as literacy grew and printing was developed.
To facilitate the above premises, Lawson asserts that,

> Printing begot newspaper and mega times which
> became strong advertising outlets, while service and
> technology soon introduced radio and cinema, and
> later television. Records of early organized
> advertising depict active agency work in Britain and
> United States of America in the mid-18th century.
> These services were a great development upon some
> form of advertising that had taken place earlier in
> countries like Germany, Austria and Holland (102).

Today, advertising and media exchange has become god and lucrative
business, with its practitioners receiving a shade of respect above the
merchants largely because of their eloquence and good turnout. The United
States of America was reputed to have had 1,400 registered advertising
agencies by 1917. Many of those agencies still exist today, although largely
renamed or restructured. In Britain, the reputation is claimed of having
produced the world's first advertising agency Reynell and Son, established in
1812 in London. From that point, advertising grew systematically and there are
reportedly about 1,10 advertising agencies in Britain today (Kaufman, 89).

Development of Nigerian Advertising and Media Exchange: A Post Modern Perspective

The earliest recorded activities that could be described as advertising in its primitive or crude form include the town crier's early morning or late evening going signals that alerted the village dwellers of an impending announcement. The going as rudimentary as it may now appear, was most effective as an attention catcher, and remains so, no matter how hard we might try to discredit it in the name of high-tech communication devices (Bel-Molokwu, 27).

Before 1982, supporting the town crier's dominance was the special emissary of the chief or village head, had the duty to often stand before the gathering at the village square to herald the day's important messages. He did it without blemish and was accurate in the task. Early crude advertising simulating acts that have been recorded in ancient Nigeria also included the use of hired individuals with the gift to voice quips about the quality of palm or grain wine, or yams. They were usually paid in kind with one or two tubers of yam or even cupfuls of wine for their services which include "advertising" the farming prowess of specific labourers whose service were available for hire during the planting season (APCON 56).

These crude forms had evolved into the hire of footmen to actually how about his quality and availability of specific goods or services by the early 19th century. Historical records exist of such footmen in various ancient Nigerian Kingdoms and Empires like Sokoto, Lagos, Benin, Ife and Kaduna. Some were hired in dual capacity, to "advertise" and to "sell". Laden with basketsful of one commodity or the other, on market days, they shouted to invite patrons to come over to them rather than the medley of other sellers. Their younger variety consisted of boys who, either for their parents or for a fee for someone else, shouted out attractive incentives in front of a mat containing wares, or ran to and fro the market entrance inviting prospective buyers to the location of the goods inside the market. Soon attention catchers like bells and whistles were introduced and with this of course came bedlam in the market places (FGNAP, 91). According to Advertising Practitioners Council of Nigeria-Advertising Education series: "The acrobatic dancers, magicians and snake charmers joined the riddle, as more attention caters like musical instruments were improved, and music transfer gadgetry developed by science" (19).

As commerce diversified, so did the urge to draw attention increase. 19th century entries like bicycles and printing brought newer scopes into the art of crude advertising. Greater mobility by the hired personnel engendered greater innovativeness by them, and creativity grew. Bicycle canvassers introduced acrobatic riding while devices like sandwich boards and posters demonstrated by fine artists caught on as forms of drawing attention. In mid-nineteenth century, the first printing press came into Lagos Nigeria following the introduction of mechanical printing in 1450 (Sam 46).

With this development, the first newspaper in Nigeria *Iwe-Irohin* was established appearing in the streets from Rev. Townsend in September, 1879. Between 1879 and 1930 provided a forum for the mostly surge of tradesmen who had hitherto organized the production of art impressions and printed posters, sandwich boards, street signs, staged events and other forms of sales promotions, the first formal media advertisement and media exchange ever carried out in Nigeria was in Iwe-Irohin and was in the form of information on shipping movement and large cargo.

Media advertising had gathered some essence facilitated by the development of modern photography in 1831 and it advent in Nigeria were landmarks by the 20th century,. Photographs, with their unique asset of image replication, brought display adverts and outdoor posters to life. Another vital medium which came into Nigeria early in the first half of the 20th century was cinema but it was not to play a role in advertising and media exchange until later on. Between 1914 and 1928 there was an upsurge in commercial activities in Nigeria, APCON-Research Department Project writes that,

> With this massive commercialization new merchandising centres developed in Kano, Calabar, Abia, Onitsha, Port-Harcourt, Benin and Lokoja, while Lagos grew beyond expectations in commercial activities and wealth creation. The Royal Niger Company metamorphosed into the Conglomerate called the United African Company (UAC) while rival houses also blossomed (51).

One of the businesses the UAC ventured into was the formation of the West African Publicity LTD which examine first advertising agency in Nigeria incorporated in London August 13th, 1928. Also the introduction of radio broadcasting in 1932 and television in 1960s, coupled with the increasing popularity of cinema, advertising and media exchange just had to grow especially with the establishment of the Western Nigeria Broadcasting Corporation (WNBC) in 1955. Advertising Practitioners Council of Nigeria "Advertising Education Series No. 3" opines that,

Cinema was utilized fully for advertising from 1950 until the popularity of celluloid film was undercut in the 1960s by the advent of television, and virtually obliterated by the advent of home videos in the late 1980s and early 1990s for film, print, outdoor, radio and all there always seems to be something to remember forever in the advertisements of the 1950s or 1960s.

Perhaps, it is as attribute of a general decline in quality, occasioned by pressures of greater and more rapid demands of today's existence, that seems to give the impression that the production men of the earlier days had all the time in the world, and the most to produce the best (APCON-Advertising Annual 99). One of the identifiable setbacks of the old advertisements appears to be deficits in manpower and technology. The effect of this foundation still affects the advertising industry today, and only recently did the country's first ever full advertising post-secondary educational facility, the APCON Diploma in Advertising Programme, begin. In terms of technology, Nigeria's lack of scientific and developmental initiative has led to the full dependence of the advertising industry on importation for all its equipment and technical support. As a result, and because some vital equipment are too costly to be acquired by one organization, users and practitioners are forced to go abroad for sophisticated productions. Bel-Mokowu asserts that,

With the oil boom of the early 1970s, and the upsurge in business turnover, advertising witnessed a spring into business. The indigenization which came in the midst of the boom was a "dues ex machina" for the advertising sector, as it was for the general investment scenario of the vibrantly rich country new force in Africa, a potential world power (24).

It is against this backdrop that new industries sprang up, including more newspapers and magazines, as well as radio and television stations which multiplied rapidly with the political restructuring of the country from three regions, through 12 states in 1967. The Nigerian Broadcasting Corporation renamed Federal Radio Corporation of Nigeria (FRCN) and the Nigerian Television Authority had, as a matter of national duty, to respond to the political and economic changes. They established stations in all the states and intensified commercial activities, faced with competition from state-owned entrepreneurship from 1975 to 1979. Facilities for colour television reception and for colour separation for process printing blossomed. Desk-top publishing computers brand new elements into the imaginative creative work in print, while sophisticated, computerized sound and video recording and reproduction innovations have greatly enriched the tonal and visual qualities of commercials on radio and television (SAM 93).

The greatest events that contributed in no small measure to the organization of advertising and the incubation of a sense of belonging to the practitioner were the birth of the Association of Advertising Practitioners of Nigeria (AAPN) in 1972, and the creation of the Advertising Practitioners Council of Nigeria (APCON) in 1989 as a statutory regulatory body for the practice of advertising and media exchange. Before the advent of the AAPN, it was virtually every man for him and advertising was all comers field. The AAPN has under its umbrella 87 corporate members, all reputable advertising agencies which believe in self-regulation as the bedrock of their practice. The AAPN has, before the advent of APCON, given the advertising practitioner a sense of pride and identity. A membership list published at the end of 1996, however, showed there were only 62 active members. To support the above ascertain, which holds that with the emergence of APCON,

> ...created by Act No. 55 of 1988, now went further to regularize advertising practice by introducing yardsticks for registration, maintenance of a register of practitioners, setting of educational standards, creation of training facilities, vetting of advertisements and publication of literature on advertising (26).

Apart from AAPN and APCON contributions to the development of modern advertising and media exchange in Nigeria, a number of other organizations have also played salient roles. They include:

- The advertisers' Association of Nigeria (AAN) in 1992. The umbrella body created by the generators of advertising, the clients, to protect their interests and to enable them has a greater voice in the state of affairs in advertising with over 30 member organizations.

- The Newspaper Proprietors Association of Nigeria (NPAN), has the responsibility of uniting the newspaper industry in the face of changing fortunes. The fore-runner of the organized media related bodies in Nigeria, the NPAN serves as a focal print for activities relating to advertising. It had 83 members at its peak, even though it is no longer very active.

- The Broadcasting Organization of Nigeria (BON-1973) is the group for radio and television houses. It has 43 member organizations.

- The Outdoor Advertising Association of Nigeria (OAAN-1985) an offshoot of the former Outdoor Advertising Contractors Association of Nigeria. It now has 48 member organizations and has been assiduous in its pursuit of standards in the outdoor sub-sector, which has the peculiar problem of proliferation of outdoor messages.

The above four associations and the AAPN form what is recognized by APCON as the sectorial groups through which it regulates the practice of advertising in the country. Directives, guideline and the Code of Advertising Practice are implemented practitioners. With the creation of APCON, modern advertising has acquired the status of a profession comparable with law, medicine, engineering and pharmacy, and penalties exist for practicing advertising without due registration.

Conclusion

In a nutshell, this paper concludes that advertising in Nigeria is as old as the Nigerian man himself, although history shows that advertising's identification as a business factor is traced from the Roman imperial periods. Due to the strong burning urge of the Nigerian man to promote his goods and services dates back to his early existence, and his advertising techniques, tactics and modes have continued to improve with technology and modernization, most especially, with the facilitation of the world-wide web and the establishment of Advertising Practioners Council of Nigeria (APCON) in1988, to provide professional educational facilities, conducting examinations in the advertising profession and awarding certificates and diplomas to successful candidates in advertising programme at the tertiary level in Nigeria.

The Advertiser' Association of Nigeria (ADVAN) 1992, to protect their interest and to enable them have a greater voice in the state of affairs in advertising. The Newspaper Proprietors Association of Nigeria (NPAN), to unite the newspaper industry in the face of changing opportunities and fortunes: The Broadcasting Organizations of Nigeria (BON), is the grouping for radio and television houses; The Outdoor Advertising Association of Nigeria (OAAN), has been assiduous in its pursuit of standards in the outdoor sub-sector.

Through the above dynamic steps in advertising and media exchange, Nigeria has witnessed tremendous and huge accomplishments in commercialization, as new merchandising centres developed in almost all parts and corners of the entire Nigerian enclave through the rapid improvement and development of the media industry. The future of advertising and media exchange in Nigeria is currently still pregnant owing to continuous developments of the media as well as the World Wide Web.

Works Cited

APCON, *Advertising Annual,* Sundry Volumes, Advertising Practitioners Council of Nigeria, Nigeria: ISBN 1117391.

APCON: Report on the study of the Advertising Practitioners Registration Degree Visa-a Vis related. Enactments", APCON Research Department Project, Undated.

Bel-Molokwu, Josef. *Principles of Advertising* APCON Advertising Education Series (No. 3) Nigeria: 2005.

_____The Nigerian Advertising Environment: Past, Present and Future Seminar Paper, Kano: July 19, 1995.

Federal Government of Nigeria, Advertising Practitioners (Registration etc). Degree and Amendments-Degree No. 55 of 1988, Degree No. 116 of 1993.

Kaufman, Louis. *Essentials of Advertising.* USA: Harcourt, Brace, Jovanovich, 2006.

Lawson, R. G. *Advertising Law.* United Kingdom: MacDonald and Evans, 1978.

Pride, M. William and Ferrel, O. C. *Marketing: Basic Concepts and Decision's* (4th Ed.), USA: Houghton Mifflin, 1985.

Sam, Ijalana O. "Advertising Practitioners Degree and other Laws Relating to Advertising in Nigeria: A Jurisdictional Study", APCON, January 6th, 1995.

TERRORISM AND EDUCATION: THE NEED FOR A PHILOSOPHY OF EDUCATION IN NIGERIA
BY
SAMUEL ASUQUO EKANEM, Ph.D
DEPARTMENT OF EDUCATIONAL FOUNDATION AND ADMINISTRATION
CROSS RIVER UNIVERSITY OF TECHNOLOGY
CALABAR – NIGERIA

ABSTRACT
In this contemporary world, terrorism has become a hazardous threat to all countries around the globe as it will cause devastating casualties and economic impact in any of the countries. Terrorism is basically an act of the terrorists to convert a message such as ideological, religious or political object through violence or destruction. The more destructive it is, the more audiences they have. As a result, the terrorists will greatly increase if they can influence people around the world to achieve the objectives or goals that the terrorists' group has plotted. This trend can be seen in the activities of Boko Haram in North East Nigeria. But education as a portent tool for social mobilization and reorientation can be effectively employed in re-engineering the social processes that produced terrorists in our world. To achieve this, the education system must be anchored on a philosophical system that will imprint in the minds of the educands certain values and thinking that will see terrorism as immoral, irrational and anti-social activity that should not exist. This paper therefore postulates that education can be a veritable means to combat and eradicate terrorism in Nigeria. This education, the paper posits, must be laid on the philosophical foundation of essencism as a philosophy of education in Nigeria.

Key-words: *Education, Terrorism, Boko Haram, Essencism, Philosophy of Education*

Introduction
The involvement of religion in national and international relations has been illustrated in various historical and modern acts of violence and wars across the globe. In recent times, attention has been focused on several acts of religious terrorism that involve self-sacrifice and murder in the name of "God". Having this in mind, it is imperative to realize that exemplary figure of faith

and major faith-based organizations have contributed significantly to social change that targets the correction of injustice and that may be seen or taken as a spiritual attempt of transforming the world into a religiously ideal one, which may implies the realization of God's kingdom" on earth.

From this, it is clear that the role of religion in both national and international affairs and relations is rather complex and complicated. The complexity here emerges from the fact that religion cannot effectively play the dual roles of promoting peace in our world and championing violence of varying dimensions and degrees. Indeed, religion cannot escape the guilty verdict of facilitating conflict, violence and terrorism in our world today. This guilty verdict of religion is premised on the dogmatic and indoctrinal process of religion as a system of belief, determined and sustained by faith. This processes of transmitting religious ideas, beliefs, dogmas and instructions made it possible for the faithfuls or adherents to be easily manipulated to follow their leader(s) blindly without questions.

The result of this religious process(es) is what the Raggae Star Bob Marley, refers to as "Mental Slavery", and this can also lead to epistemic disorientation of the mind. What can naturally emerge as ideas through this process will only be warped, distorted and misunderstood system. This then present us a vivid picture of the platonic "allergory of the cave" where the faithfuls or adherents only see any form of illumination through the eye of their leaders, who often times interpret scriptural injunctions and doctrines as deterministic without the possibility of human choice that can be achieved through freewill.

So, the imprisoned or caged minds of the faithfuls or adherents can only be liberated through education that illuminate the minds and therefore breaks the chains of ignorance created through religious indoctrination and dogmaticisim. This educative process is anchored on the Socratic dictum that ignorance is "vice" while knowledge is a "virtue". These point to the fact that terrorism is a product of ignorance and to eradicate this vice, we need to go through the virtuous path of education. This educative process that must be pursued must basically be laid on certain principles that are philosophical. It is on the basis of this that this paper advocates for Essencism as a philosophy of Education that will help Nigeria eradicate terrorism.

Causes and Effects of Terrorism

In our world today, terrorism has become a mortal danger and a threat that require multi-sectoral approach to find a solution. The reason for this is because terrorism is still very active around the world, and the causes of this dreadful act that harm several people's lives and properties is due mostly to the formation of nationalist, separalist or fundamentalist groups. This nationalist formation is traceable to colonialism as nationalist movement has very high chances of becoming a terrorist organization. History is repletes with violence opposition of colonialism as Mahatma Ghandi was the only one that gets along with the freedom movement without any violenct act. Extreme nationalism according to Wikipedia (2014) "upholds language rights, religious beliefs and symbols. They persuade on a regional-ethic party and accentuate on the political rights and priviledges" (1).

Also, resistance against an oppressor is a serious factor that can contribute to terrorism. The dominance of terrorists' land and their people from any oppressor have high apparent high chances of conducting terrorism. Here we can see the IRA, the Basque separatist group ETA, The Palestinians, the Tamil Tigers, the Chechans, and Iraqi insurgents are certain examples of organization that employed forces to fulfill their political goals (Wikipedia, 2014).

Social stratification and disproportion of the division of limited resources such as food, water and clothing has been considered a major factor that relates terrorism. In a study Keet (2003), reveals that lack of economic management provides huge impact on civilian for their survival needs. Based on this study Keet (2003) holds that fifteen (15%) percent of the population of the poor countries consumes eighty five percent (85%) of the overall resources. As a result, Keet (2003) states that if these group of people cannot get a satisfactory amount of resources they require, there is every likelihood that they will use force or violence to get what they want as to remain alive. So, these circumstances of deprived or lack of socio-economic conditions can lead to the formation of new society or organization that can bring about terrorism. It is on the basis of this that most scholars classified Boko Haram in Northern Nigeria. The argument is that it is the socio-economic conditions created in the north by political leaders that generate or create the enabling environment for Boko Haram to strive. This logic is supported by the fact that Boko Haram recruits its members and fighters through financial inducement.

There is also the contradictory of theory of disaffected intelligentsia that is simple minded people that kind of lack moral and social knowledge as being one of the causes of violence and terrorism. These provide reason that dehumanizes terrorists and as such they want to be heard, and acknowledged by the society or the world, that they also have the equivalent of human rights.

This provides the inner reason of terrorism, decreeing from their perspectives, mindset, and method of approach and the consequences of their activities (Wikipedia, 2014; Lincoln, 2003).

Apart from the dehumanization of terrorists, it is a fact that religion is a fundamental cause of terrorism as can be seen in the Muslim extremists in the middle east, ISIS in Iraq and even Boko Haram in Northern Nigeria. Islamic terrorism as typified by ISIS and Boko Haram rejects the ideology of and individualism, dislike the concept of capitalism, Western Education and solely believe in Caliphate (which is the idea of leading Muslim Community Worldwide). It is the belief of people that social issue was connected to the war, but religion in Keet (2003) studies indicates that different belief have a higher chance to engage in a battle than those that share the same belief.

Another study by Borum (2004), revealed that most terrorists behaved the way they do as a result of perceived injustice, wanted identity, and these people were target victims of terrorism. Traumatizes from their childhood as a result of abuse, they felt injustice as well as humiliated, and these, they joined the terrorists' group as they are majority in the group. So, people that search for the terrorist organization in several ways as one of them referred to "identity foreclosure", when the idea of or mindset of a terrorist organization is accepted without any serious reflective activity or question. These youths usually accept the mindset as they could no longer take the complexity and stressful world, and these group of persons are usually classified as lifeless or monotonous person (Wikipedia, 2014; Cardinal, Hallos Eventh 2002).

It is on the basis of this that the chibok girls and other kidnapped persons by Boko Haram are seen by some as potential threat to terrorism in Nigeria, when they are eventually rescued. Their rescue should be followed by serious psychological work to alter their mindset before they are fully integrated into the society. This can only be achieved through education.

Again, motivation of the terrorists is the tap-root of terrorism. Motive here is viewed as the passion of aspiration to get something done. The chance to get into action, the belonging needs, the wish to get acknowledgment of material and spiritual rewards are the motivations to get involve in terrorism. For instance, Boko Haram recruits get as much as four hundred dollars on recruitment and this is a clear case of material reward. There is also the idea that any on the dies in the cause of Islamic terrorism will go to heaven and will be given seven virgins as wives, and most of these recruits are motivated to get such spiritual reward for their terrorist acts, hence the high incidences of suicide bombers. This cannot not be without a high indoctrination of these suicide bombers (Fredland, 1992).

Furthermore, the remedies of an injustice could be a basic motivation for terrorism as this can help them revenge, and help others to achieve vengeance as well. The need for a sense of belonging has a great impact on radical extremist groups as they felt connected and associated with the group. So, social defiant that were expelled and rejected from their society but accepted by the group will certainly feel a sense of warmth and kindness just like we have in a family (Cardinal, Parkinson, Hallad and Everitt, 2007).

From our analysis, the causes of terrorism in our world today are somewhat unavoidable; however, the effects of terrorism are on the tourism industry. Just after the incident of 9/11, the impact on world travel and tourism council reported that over ten percent (10%) of the travel and tourism demand world wide drastically reduced and as a result about 8.8 million people lost their job in airlines, hotels, tour operators, car rentals, and credit card companies, and so there was a decrease of 1.7% of total Gross Domestic Product (GDP) of the world economy (Wikipedia, 2014). Indeed, the attacks on the world Trade Centre affected seriously international arrivals around the world in 2001, which showed a decrease of 4million less than that of 2000 and this showed that people were scared of taking flights, and this have serious negative consequences on airlines companies as the number of passengers were on the decrease (Hoffman, 1998; Hoffman, 2003).

In Nigeria, the economic effects of terrorists' activities by Boko Haram are enormous. Indeed, the economies of the north eastern states of Borno, Yobe and Adamawa in Nigeria are in shamble. A lot of lives and properties have been lost due to terrorist attacks by Boko Haram. The Federal Government spent billions of Naira in an effort to contend the insurgency of Boko Haram. Presently, the Federal Government is to borrow one Billion US Dollars to enable the government fight terrorism. These are enormous resources that would have been used for other developmental purposes in the country. This has also affected the influx of investment into Nigeria, especially in the north eastern part of Nigeria.

In the market and parks, people are devastated by terrorist acts as human tragedies occurred often times. Due to fear, several people refused to take the risk of starting a business as terrorism could strike any time, anywhere and so bring down the economy. Also, the costs that take care of security has become a big burden to companies and these has brought about a decrease in the price of stock. Indeed, labour has been lost due to terrorism and this have negative effects on the companies and the nation's economy (Gambotta, 2005).

The economy around the world has been negatively affected due to act of terrorism. The capital stock, either in physical or human form, has been greatly reduced due to terrorists' act. The productive industries are not spared the effect of terrorism. (Sandler and Enders, 2001).

Apart from the economy, terrorism also affect the school system as can be seen in the Chibok girls adopted by Boko Haram in Borno in north east Nigeria. This incidence caused the closure of schools in the state, and the academic calendar seriously disrupted. Furthermore, the spiritual life of the people is seriously affected as most people are afraid to go to places of worship, which have suddenly become prime target of terrorists' assault and destruction.

Terrorism and Education

Through our discourse on the causes and effects of terrorism, we discovered that terrorism is carried out by people for several reasons. Although, it is the view that terrorism is unavoidable, but it can be drastically reduced if not eradicated through education. Indeed, education can assist to show potential terrorists that there is a better way to engaged with the world. This should be the focus and struggle in this 21st century. This is because, terrorism cannot be defeated until there are a combined effort to fight its root causes as well as it ghastly and devastating consequences. Today, in our world, is an art that stretches from the Far East, through the Middle East to the streets of cities in Europe, the United States and Africa, as we are confronted with a scourge and a monster that has taken innocent lives, scarred communities especially in North East Nigeria and established countries. Terrorism has become a threat that is ever evolving, growing and mutating to counter our fight against it.

The extremists and fundamentalists propagating this violence have serious networks of outreach to the young people and are very much aware of the power of education, whether formal or informal; hence, they fill the young minds with beliefs that anyone who disagrees is an enemy and equally an enemy of God. The state as usual focused on the consequences as states always consider immediate security measures after every attack, and this involves hunting down terrorists and thereafter we return to our daily lives until there is another attack.

This is a very wrong approach to the problem of terrorism, because lasting change depends on dealing with the root causes of extremism and fundamentalism. It is a fact that politics play a role, and these terrorists are very good at jumping on the back of political grievances. The real soil in which they plant the seeds of hate is wonderfully fertilized with ignorance.

It is as a result of this that we need to start thinking of education as a relevant and potent security issue. The extremist provide justification for killing in the name of God. This is as obscene and clear perversion of actual religious faith. It is a serious menace, for both the harm it does directly and for the damaging division and sectarianism that it nurtures indirectly. Every killing as we know it is a human tragedy, but these also cause a chain reaction of bitterness and hatred. This generates real fear in the communities plagued by terrorism, fear that paralyzed normal life as we have in North East Nigeria, and pushes people away from each other (Hammy 1998, Freeman, 1996).

Globalization promotes the intensification and multiplication of terrorism due to extremism. There exists no borders as this can spring up anywhere without warning or the danger sign. Presently, we are connected more closely than other time in human history as more people come in contact with those who are different from them. This social process engendered by globalization should make it possible for us to respect our neighbour who is not just like us. This also presents to us the capacity and the scope to identify his or her as an enemy at a greater level.

This is not only about Islamic extremism as there are extremist acts carried out against Muslims due largely to their religion, and there are also fanatical Christians, Jews, Hindus and Buddlists that disfigure the true nature of their faith. This scenario therefore makes a education vital and potent 21st century security issue for all of us. What we need to focus on is to prove and show young people that there are vulnerable to appeals from terrorists that there is a better path to have their voice heard, and a more meaningful and effective manner to engage with the world, (Ehrlich, 1973).

We indeed know how to do this as we need to design a school programme that will promote cross-cultural dialogue among students from the age of 9-18 around the world. Students should be reached through well trained teachers around the world to teach the values of tolerance and respect for the other person's belief, views, ways of life, among others. Pupils right from the primary schools should be exposed to the belief that no religion is supreme. Religion as a matter of fact, should be made to be seen as strictly subjective experience that should never interfere with the right and lives of other people.

At the secondary and tertiary level of education, students should be engaged to discuss global issues from a variety of faith and belief perspectives. This will enable them to gain the requisite dialogue skills needed to prevent conflict through the breaking down of religious and cultural stereotypes. This process can be achieved through the Internet and other facilitating methods so as to access and engage all young people even in the poorest stage.

Conflict resolution and peace education should be made more practical oriented within the school curriculum. We need to mobilize the young people and everybody to defeat extremism. This can best be achieved education where the sanctity and sacredness of human life is raised to global, or universal, national and local way of life.

This view of using education is supported by Tony Blair in a speech he presented at the United Nations Assembly in January 2014. He argued that education should be made a security issue in world in the 21st century. He illustrated the potency and practicability of this with his faith foundation, where the school programme promotes cross-cultural dialogue through facilitated video conferences with the help of trained teachers that help the young people to see global and religious issues in a more objective and logical manner, rather than from the perspective of religion or culture.

It is on the strength of this that education should be seen as a fundamental security issue, and this should not be any kind of education but education that specifically designed to open young mind to the other, that is, those who are culturally and religiously different, and show than how the only future that works is the one in which people are respected as equals whatever their faith or culture.

The need for Philosophy of Education: Essecism as a Proposal.

A cursory look at the causes and effects of terrorism in this discourse portray ignorance as a fundamental reason for people to go into violent acts, crime and terrorism. So, for ignorance as a vice to be cured or eradicated from our world generally, and Nigeria in particular, there is the urgent need for massive education of the young minds as already canvassed here. This education however, must be anchored on a specific philosophical foundation that will aid the proper engineering of the young minds. But the question is; why philosophy of education?

Nwankubor (2009) tends to provide an answer to the above question when he writes:

> The recognition of the role of philosophy and education in influencing ideas, opinions, judgments and attitudes to life and living in general. That Philosophy and education hold sway in the

development and under-development, Shaping and reshaping, construction and reconstruction, of the face of existence cannot be doubted in the light of keen examination of the existential pendulum. What may no be so obvious to some people is how Philosophy and education direct the entire wheel of existence. A little examination of the conventional history of human societies and evolution of social institutions, will convince one of the tremendous importance of philosophy and education in the making of "change and permanence" in existential realities (xvi).

What can be gleaned from this is the fact that philosophy and education are the results upon which the wheel of life, development and social transformation rotates. This is so because human and social values that mould the norms and morals of social existence can only be evolved and produce through philosophy and education. It is through philosophy that a pattern or system and logic of the thoughts process that generate he norms and morality of human existence can be synchronized and produced. It is through philosophy that the values derivable from education can be rationalized and justified as a worthwhile activity or not. It is this craves for rationalization and justification that make philosophy of education the most valuable vehicle of social transformation through the vital change agent or human mind.

Again, philosophy of education is required because human society "needs reconstruction, recreation, true integral and sustainable development, before the ark of existence sinks beneath the abyss" (Ozumba, 2009). Humanity according to Ozumba (2009) "needs to reestablish its 'existential status quo, if it is not to suffer 'ontological eclipse". Terrorism as carried out today in Nigeria by Boko Haram and al Queda in other parts of the world can bring about the sudden esclipse of humanity, hence, we need a philosophy of education that can drives the educative process through existential and essencist value orientation. For as Ozumba (2009) puts it, it is only philosophy and education that can "lead humanity out of the present mess (we find ourselves) and thereby avoiding the regret of falling into abysmal existential cataclysm". Indeed, with true philosophy and a sound education in the mold of Essencism as we are going to advocate here the glory of existence would flower for the "common good", and man will be reconnected to the divine source of life and peace. (Ekanem, 2005).

Philosophy of education portrays or highlights the level of sense and meaning that education can make, as it also provides clarification in education. This is because, education without philosophy is aimless, directionless and poinous. So education as the process of transmitting ideas or knowledge, can only be desirable or worthwhile to the individual members of the society if it grounded in a philosophy. It is therefore, on the basis of this that we proposed Essencism as a philosophy of Education that can help Nigeria and the world to defect terrorism permanently. But before we outline the relevance importance and values of this philosophy it is pertinent we define it.

Essencism as a philosophy is a coinage derived from the word "essence" which means what "makes a thing what it is" (Hornby 2000). It is a philosophy proposed by Ekanem (2005) in a Doctoral dissertation titled "A Philosophy of Edcation for Technological Development in Nigeria". This philosophy seeks to highlight the essence of man on planet earth. The reason for this particular philosophy is the need to evolve entirely a home grown philosophy of education that will cater for the peculiar needs of Nigeria. Again, the foreign philosophies "imported" into Nigeria such as idealism, naturalism, realism and pragmatism tend to diminish the importance of the essence of man as the controller of the habitable earth. Most of these philosophies make serious efforts to disconnect man from his Creator and nature. These also seeks to dehumanize and alienate man hence, essencism as a philosophy becomes an imperative as it sees man as the centrality of all the happenings on earth. Man here, is seen as the deteminant and designer of the world that he lives and controls. This is anchored on the fact that right from the biblical epoch, man was given the divine authority to inherit the earth and dominate it. In Genesis, we are made to understand that God created man in His own image to have both physical and spiritual dominion over all things. So, as the last thing that God created before His rest, man represents the Divine Authority of God. Man therefore is God's ambassador and as an ambassador, man enjoys high degree of immunity and so are protected from being harmed by anything on earth (Ekanem, 2005).

This implies that man is imbued with divine intelligence and knowledge, that assist him to fulfill God's purpose on earth. It follows then that man's education must strive to establish this essence that is, those vital qualities that make man who he is by God. These essential qualities of man can be seen in the dual nature of man as both physical and spiritual being. This dualism is the hallmark of man's essence. So, any philosophy or idea that attempts to diminish or de-emphasis this dualism must be rejected. Man was created for a divine purpose of sustaining the earth and promoting existence through procreation. Man was created for the purpose of dominating his environment as put in place by God. Therefore, mans' stay in the Garden of Eden was to provide him with a period of divine education that will empower and enable him cope and dominate his environment outside the garden. This domination of the environment does not include terrorism that seek to destroy man and the environment. It follows here that terrorism is antithetical to the divine will of God, as it concerns man's essence.

This clearly shows that historically, the education of man was divinely designed to reflect his techno-nature. This manifest itself in the ability of man to provide names to all things created by God without duplication. As a result of this, it can be argued that the education of man is divinely inspired. This inspirational dimension of education seeks to satisfy the spiritual essence of man, while the applied science-technology actualized the physical manifestation of man's spiritual development. The implied meaning of this is that it is the spiritual foundation of education that can inspire real development anchored on the principle of who man really is. It is this spiritual development that can lead effortlessly to the technological. This then satisfies the physical essence of man since it is through technological advancement that man is provided with his physical comfort. But for even the physical comfort to be achieved or attained there must be a corresponding spiritual level of development. Inclusive in this spiritual aspect or man's essence, is the ethical value for all that is good. It provides man with a sound knowledge of what is good and bad. This knowledge which essencism will provide will conform to the Socratic character of virtue, which will make it possible as a socio-cultural practice that honesty pays. It will also help to wipe of the culture and practice of hatred, looting of the national, state and local government treasuries through public office. This essencist education will provide the necessary knowledge for respect for human life, and will introduce a balanced view of religion man, God, belief, economy, politics etc and delineate basic characteristics that will establish different domains for each. This delineation will prevent the cobweb-view that generate and create tension and conflict when it comes to religion. The attainment of these socio-cultural reforms through essencism is because the dual aspect of every citizen will be developed through this educational philosophy. This is because as a spirit being, man is directly linked with God from where the source of his intellectual inspiration is derived.

The spiritual development of man through essencism will re-establish a direct link with God. And when God is involved in the affairs of man, we can be sure that harmony will be established, and development is bound to occur with much case.

As a philosophy, essencism seeks to develop a complete human personality. This is because no aspect of the human nature or aspect is ignored. Through essencism man is totally developed as a physical and as a spiritual being. This is anchored on the firm belief that it is when the human personality is completely developed that one can begin to talk of other aspects of development. This is due to the fact that the development of any nation is dependent upon the development of the human person. Omoregbe (1990) agrees with this assertion when he states that "The most important aspect of the development of any country is indisputably the development of the human personality. It is, in other words, the moral development of the citizens that constitute the country…" (147).

Indeed, a morally developed personality will not be involved in the acts of terrorism, neither can he contemplate suicide bombing so as to die and be rewarded with "Virgins". It is only ignorance due to lack of sound education and philosophy that can make people to be conscripted into terrorist group like Boko Haram. It is through essencism therefore, that the mis-education, mis-envision and the "the "Deschooling Society" can be achieved. This is because Nigerians and Africans have been schooled to believe that what is good for Europe is good for us and what is good for us is archaic or outmoded and uncivilized if they are not from Europe". (Illich, 1972; Ozumba, 2009).

It is on the basis of this that Nigeria and other African states or nations institutionalized values which according to Ozumba (2009) "have neither help us to be qualitatively good… nor to be our unique selves contributing a ray of beautiful colors to the lay-sack colors emitted by various nations who pursue a philosophy of education that is tailored to meet their unique needs" (8)

Essencism as a home-grown philosophy is comprehensive and strategic to fill the identified gap so identified by Ozumba. And as a philosophy of education it is sound enough to satisfy the criteria of Durosaro (1988) who maintain that a sounds philosophy of education is anchored on an adequate philosophy
of life.

This is because philosophy of education is all about the goods that education is attempting to accomplish and the reasons for which schools at the different levels were established. Essencism as a philosophy of education adequately satisfies the four identified aspects of philosophy of education, which includes; education as a bridge between the past and the present that shares the future; education as a tool for social change and development, and then, education as a personal function. The implication of this is that any worthwhile, progressive philosophy of education that can engender development must necessarily recognize the culture, the past, the present and the future of the society; such philosophy must also be involved in the adaption of social changes and the holistic development of the individual.

These, essencism seeks to achieved as it is a combination of physical and spiritual dimensions of man into a whole that will create a unique system, character and culture in the Nigerian state through education. This combination will help the country in the fight against terrorism as it will emphasis the sanctity of human life and establish a national culture of peaceful co-existence, with existential tenets that can promote development. This is because man is God's project and it is only that divine direction that illuminates the spirit of man that bring about knowledge, that can practically solve man's physical problems, which include terrorism, socio-economic deprivation, religious acrimony, injustice, ethnicity etc. The secret of man's latent power and potentials is discoverable in essencism that provides a kind of education that places man at the very centre, and its basic principles can only be discovered, defined, interpreted and applied by man.

Conclusion

Efforts have been made to discuss terrorism and education in this paper. We established the difficulty encountered in providing universally acceptable definition of terrorism. Also, the causes and effects of terrorism was elaborately discussed. With the causes and effects of terrorism understood, and the consequences of this on Nigeria, we proposed that education that is laid on a sound philosophy can effectively tackled the problem of terrorism in Nigeria, Africa and the world. In our search, essencism was seen as a philosophy of education that can adequately bring about a kind of citizenry that will make terrorism irrelevant and unacceptable in the country. The reason for the adoption of essencism as a philosophy of education is seen in its potency to develop the physical and spiritual aspects of man that enhance the moral quality of the citizenry.

There has been a great reservoir of ignorance on the part of the people hence, the various acts of violence and terrorism. And since there exists no philosophy of education in Nigeria, we made a systematic effort to advocate for a truly home grown philosophy, which is Essencism. This philosophy seeks to evolve and design a national focus that is reflective of the real nature of man as a dual being. This dualism is clearly expressed in the mind-body interactional principle. So, essencism as a philosophy of education seeks to justify the divine importance of education. This is because; the dualistic nature of man is nobly catered for through the physical and spiritual dimensions. And once there is harmony between the physical and spiritual, terrorism will escape the consciousness of Nigerians, not withstanding the religious inclination of the citizens, *and the Biblical prophesy of "my people perish from lack of knowledge" (Hosea 4:6)*will not be fulfilled in the country through terrorism.

Work Cited

Akorta, C. and R. Sosis (2005) "Ritual, emotion, and sacred symbols: The evolution of religion as an adaptive complex." *Human Nature* 16:323-359

Argo, N. (2003) "The banality of evil! Understanding today's human bombs". *Policy paper. Preventive Defense Project.* Standard University.

Bering, J. (2006) "The cognitive psychology of belief in the supernatural" *American Scientist* 94:142-149

Cardinal, R. J. Pakinson, J., Hall, J. and Everitt, B. (2002) "Emotion and Motivation". The role of the anygada, ventran striatum and prefrontal cortex. Neuroscience and Biobehavioural Reviews.

Durosaro, I. A. and Durosaro, D. O. 1988 *Philosophical Foundations of Education*, Ibadan Odua printing Co. Ltd.

Ekanem, S. A. (2005) "A philosophy of education for technological development in Nigeria" A Doctoral (Ph.D) Dissertation, University of Calabar, Nigeria.

Ehrlich, I. (1973) "Participation in illegitimate activities: A Theoretical and Empirical Investigation". The Journal of Political Economy, May 1973, 81(3): 521-565.

Freeman, R. (1996) "Why Do so many young American Men Commit Crimes and What Might We Do About It? Journal of Economic Perspectives 10(1), Winter 1996:25-42

Friedland, N. (1992) "Becoming A Terrorist: social and individual Antecedents" In Terrorism: Roots, Impact, Responses, L. Howard, Ed. New York: praceger, pp. 81-93

Gambetha, D. (2005) Making sense of Suicide Mission Oxford: Oxford University Press.

Hamm, M. S. (998) "Terrorism, Hate, Crime and Antigovernment Violence: A Review of the Research" In Harvey N. Kusher, Ed. The Future of Terrorism: Violence in the New Millennium London, SAGE, Pp 59 – 96.

Hoffman, B. (1998), Inside Terrorism. New York: Columbia University Press.

Hoffman, B. (2003). "The logic of suicide Terrorism" The Atlantic Monthly 291:40.

Illich, I. (1972). *Deschooling Society.* New York: Harper and Row publishers.

Lincoln, B. (2003), Holy Terrors: Thinking About religion after September 11, Chicago: University of Chicago press.

Omoregebe, J. I. (1990) Knowing Philosophy Lagos: Joja Educational Research and publishing.

Ozumba, G.O., Obinagu, Q.I. and Nwankwor, I.J. (2009), Philosophy and Education in the Third Millennium AD Anambra: Verax global.

Sandler, T. and Enders, W. (2001) "An economic perspective on transnational terrorism" Mimeo., University of Southern California.

Wikipedia, 2014.

Journal of Integrative Humanism – Ghana: Vol. 4 No. 1, October, 2014, ISSN: 2026-6286

BOKO HARAM: A LEGAL AND BIBLICAL PERSPECTIVE
BY
FRANCIS FELIX EDET, Ph.D
DEPARTMENT OF RELIGIOUS AND CULTURAL STUDIES
UNIVERSITY OF CALABAR

ABSTRACT

Boko Haram-the nickname means: "Western Education is Sinful or Forbidden" believes western influences have corrupted Nigerian society and want to install an Islamic State under strict Shariah law. The sect has evolved from a local insurgency to a brutal militant group and an international terrorist group. It is an incontrovertible fact that violence linked to the Boko Haram insurgency has tremendously escalated and has resulted in several deaths, numbering thousands between 2002 and 2014.Boko Haram, which was founded in 2002 initially, focused on opposing Western Education. Boko Haram has launched military operations in 2009 to create an Islamic State. Thousands have been killed as a result of the operation of this sect. The sect has also attacked police and UN headquarters in Abuja.Boko Haram is not only a Local terrorist organization, it has a ring of international connections associated with it. This paper intents to examine the effect of Boko Haram on Nigeria as a country. It will also examine the position of the law and Bible on the issue of Boko Haram as well as the useful steps that can be taken to eradicate subsequent attacks by the sect. The Holy writ and law has something to say regarding this issue. There are also several steps that can be taken by government to curb the activities of this sect. This paper shall examine these issues.

Key-words: *Boko Haram, Shariah law, Bible, Western Education, Islam*

The Meaning, History and Activities of Book Haram

The congregation of the people of Tradition for proselytism and Jihad – better known by its Hausa name Boko Haram - is an Islamic Jihadist Militant Organization or sect based in the Northern part of Nigeria. It is an extremist Islamic sect in Nigeria that has created havoc across the Northern part of Nigeria.

The group which refers to itself as "Jama'atu Ahl as Sunnah li-Da'awati Wai-Jihad" (JASD) or group of the sunni has attacked Nigeria's police, military, rival clerics, politicians, schools, religious buildings, public institutions and civilians with increasing regularity since 2009. These attacks intensified at different times in the country.

Boko Haram is said to have been created in 2002 in Maiduguri, the capital of the Northern State of Borno, by Islamic cleric Mohammed Yusuf, who led a group of radical Islamist youth in the 1990s. The group aims at establishing a fully Islamic state in Nigeria, including the implementation of criminal Sharia courts across the country.

History has shown that Yusuf was a trained Salafist (a school of thought often associated with Jihad, and was strongly influenced by Ibn Taymiyyah, a fourteenth-century legal scholar who preached Islamic fundamentalism and is an important figure for radical groups in the Middle East (Lubeck 5). It is this background of his that gave birth to the Islamic sect called Boko Haram.

The sect is committed to the propagation of the prophet's teaching and Jihad. It colloquially translates into "Western Education is sin". The sect rejects all western concepts and condemns them as evil.

It is also said that before 2009, the group had no intention of violently overthrowing the government. Yusuf criticized northern Muslims for participating in what he saw as an illegitimate non-Islamic state; and preached the doctrine of withdrawal. But violent clashes between Christians and Muslims and harsh government treatment including pervasive police brutality, encourage the group's radicalization.

Nigeria assembled a joint Task Force (JTF) of military and police unit to battle Boko Haram and declared a "state of emergency" in three northeast states – Borno, Yobe and Adamawa, in May 2013. The move pushed the militants out of cities, but attacks in rural areas continued.

Some fighters of this sect claim to have been trained in Iran and are part of a Shite Muslim group (Zenni 12). Zenni also noted that many foot soldiers of this group are drawn from improvished religiously uneducated youth.

Ngwodo, writing about Boko Haram has noted that:

> The emergence of Boko Haram signifies the maturation of long – festering extremist impulses that run deep in the social reality of northern Nigeria. But the group itself is an effect and not a cause; it is a symptom of decades of failed government and elite delinquency finally ripening into social chaos (Ngwodo 10).

Boko Haram has used the growing grievances to promote the idea that an Islamic state would bring a better and more just government to power. Its origins appear to be rooted in grievances over poor governance and sharp inequality in Nigerian society.The following is a Chronology of attacks by Boko Haram since 2003:

1.   On the 23rd December, 2003, a group of about 200 Boko Haram Militants launched attacks on police stations in the towns of Kanamma and Geidam in Yobe state from their enclave outside Kanamma on the Nigeria border with Niger. Boko Haram killed several policemen and requisitioned police weapons and vehicles. Following the deployment of military troops to handle the insurrection, 18 Boko Haram members were killed and a good number arrested.

2.   On the 23rd of September, 2004 Boko Haram militants attacked police stations in the towns of Gwoza and Bama in Borno State, killing four policemen and two civilians. They took to the Mandaram Mountains along the Nigeria Cameroon border. Soldiers and two gunships were deployed in the mountains and after two days of battle 27 sect members were killed while the rest escaped.

3.   On the 10th of October, 2014 Boko Haram attacked a convoy of 60 policemen in an ambush near the town of Kala Balge on the border with Chad. The militants took 12 policemen hostage and police authorities presumed they were killed by the gunmen because all attempts to trace them proved abortive.

4.   From 2005 – 2008, Boko Haram went underground, reducing its attacks and focusing on recruiting new members and storing up resources.

5.   On the 7th of September, 2010 a group of Boko Haram gunmen freed over 700 inmates including around 100 sect members from a prison in Bauchi. Four people including a soldier, one policeman and two residents were killed in the raid.

6.   On the 24th – 27th of December 2010, a series of attacks claimed by Boko Haram militants in the central city of Jos and Maiduguri killed at least of 86 persons.

7.   On the 29th December, 2010 suspected Boko Haram gunmen shoot dead eight people in Maiduguri, including the governorship candidate of the ruling All Nigerian Peoples Party (ANPP) in Borno State.

8.   On the 27th of May, 2011, a group of around 70 suspected Boko Haram gunmen killed eight people including four policemen in simultaneous gun and bomb attacks on a police station, a police barracks and in Damboa, Borno State, near the border with Chad.

9.   On the 29th of May, 2011, three bombs rip through a beer garden in a military barracks in northern city of Bauchi killing 13 and wounding 33 persons.

10.   On the 7th of June, 2011, an attack on a church and two police posts in Maiduguri, initiated by Boko Haram militants, left at least 14 dead.

11.   On the 16th of June 2011, Boko Haram targets national police headquarters in Abuja, killing two.

12.   On the 20th of June, 2011 seven people, including five policemen killed in a gun and bomb attacks on a police station and a bank in Kankara, Kastina State.

13.   On the 27th of June, 2011 Boko Haram gunmen and bomb attacked a beer garden in Maiduguri, leaving at least 25 dead and dozens injured.

14.   On the 25th of August, 2011 gun and bomb attacks by Boko Haram on two police stations and two banks in Gombi, Adamawa State killed several people.

15.   On the 26th August, 2011 Boko Haram claims responsibility for a suicide bomb blast on the UN compound in Abuja, killing 23 people.

16.   On the 4th of September, 2011, Muslim Cleric, Malam Dala Shot dead by two Boko Haram members outside his home in the Zinnari area of Maiduguri.

17.   On the 12th of September, 2011, seven men, including four police men, were killed by Boko Haram gunmen in bomb and shoot attacks on a police station and a bank in Migau, Bauchi State. The attackers also robbed the bank.

18.   On the 13th of September, 2011, four soldiers shot and wounded in an ambush by Boko Haram members in Maiduguri shortly after the arrest of 15 sect members in military raids on Boko Haram hide outs in the city.

19.   On the 3rd of October, 2011 three killed in Boko Haram attacks on Baga market in Maiduguri, Borno State. The victims included a tea seller, a drug store owner and a passerby.

20.   On the 1st of October, 2011, a butcher and his assistant are killed by Boko Haram gunmen at Baga market in Maiduguri in a targeted killing.

21.   On January, 2012, Boko Haram launched a bomb attack and heavy gun battle in Kano, targeting the police headquarters. Over 150 people reported killed.

22.   On January, 2012, President Goodluck Jonathan says Boko Haram has infiltrated government, including executive national assembly and the Judiciary.

23.   In January 2012, President Goodluck Jonathan declared a State of emergency in 15 local Government areas in Borno, Yobe and Plateau State.

24.   On the 17th of September 2013, Boko Haram attacked Banisheikh, 74 kilometers west of Maiduguri, killed at least 142 people and was the most lethal incident in Borno State, since 2010.

25.   On the 14th of April, 2014 Boko Haram released a bomb in Nyanya, Abuja. The explosion killed more than 70 people and left more than 100 people wounded.

26.   On the 15th of April 2014, Boko Haram Militant attacked Chibok in Borno State, Nigeria, abducted more than 276 female students (www.ngex.com/nigeria/bokoharam/htm).

Boko Haram and the Bible

Apparently, the Bible is totally against killing. In **Exodus 20:13**, the Bible says: "Thou shall not kill". This scripture completely condemns killing of any kind. This same scripture is repeated in **Deuteronomy 5:17**: "Thou shall not kill" and in **Matthew 5:21**: "ye have heard that it was said by them of old time. Thou shall not kill. And whosoever shall kill shall be in danger of the judgment". The Bible therefore condemns killing outrightly. Judged from this perspective, the constant killing of people in the name of Boko Haram is unscriptural… Life is God-given; and should not be taken with impunity.

It is not proper for an adherent of any religion to advocate the fact that they have been permitted to kill in the name of propagating a religion. Such a teaching is absurd and uncanny. Life must be highly respected. Stressing the importance of life, **Igwe** noted that: "There is a wider and compressive respect for life as it does not only imply that life be not taken but as that it be maintained" (39).

To kill another person is to have a guilty conscience. God expect our conscience to be offence-free. Emphasizing this, Uduigwomen noted that:

> God expects us to have "A conscience void of offence toward God and men" **(Act 24 vs 16)** . An offence –free conscience involves an inner freedom of spirit that comes when we know that God is not offended by our thoughts and actions **(Acts 23:1, I Tim. 1:5)**. When a good conscience is corrupted by sin, one's faith, prayer life and relationship with God are adversely affected **(I Tim 1:15, 16) (185)** .

The essence of man's life is having a pure and undefiled relationship with God. When this relationship is not in place, then everything else cannot function adequately. Man is created to relate with his creator. This relationship is not possible when a person is a killer and murderer.

Boko Haram and the Law

St. Thomas Aquinas (1225 - 1274), easily the most eminent theologian and philosopher of the high middle ages gave his classical definition of law as follows: "Law is nothing else than an ordinance of reason for the common good, promulgated by him who has care of the community". (Cited in Iwe 22). Similarly **Justice Oputa** has noted that: "The law may then in this sense be defined as command enforced by some sanction, a rule of action to which men are obliged or are under obligation to make their conduct conformable" (2). **Graneris**a professor of philosophyof law has noted that: "Law is a social and enforce able ordinance of human action according to the criterion of justice" (25). I will add that: Law is a rational, legal and enforceable social ordinance, authoritatively promulgated, for the achievement of the common good of all members of the society, in consonant with the standard of justice.

Law as an ordinance indicates that law is not merely an advice, counsel or suggestion but rather an order, a command and a directive of the law maker to the members of the society. Law as an ordinance must be rational and reasonable.

The purpose of law therefore is to protect society and protect the citizens by creating the social conditions for the reign and development of the dignity of man and his fundamental rights and freedom. This essential purpose of law is achieved through the creation of adequate social, political, cultural and educational institutions.

Justice, which is one of the cardinal virtues of morality, is a critical criterion of law. Every law must pass the critical ethical test of justice, if it is to generate an adequate moral binding force on the members of the society.

The constitution of the Federal Republic of Nigeria provides that no person shall be deprived intentionally of his life save in execution of the sentence of a court in respect of a criminal offence of which he has been found guilty. The criminal code renders it thus: "It is unlawful to kill any person unless such killing is authorized or justified or excused by law" (Sec 306). Similarly, in section 315, the criminal code says: "Any person who unlawfully kills another is guilty of an offence which is called murder or manslaughter, according to the circumstances of the case". Also, section 319 says: "subject to the provisions of this section any person who commits the offence of murder shall be sentenced to death". The law therefore sees in all beings in possession of human life as worthy of its care and charity. The law in this sense seeks to protect human life from inhuman treatment and from the dangers to which the sacredness of life is exposed. Here, the law upholds the fundamental dignity of all human lives.

The right to live is the most fundamental of all human rights. It is a right which springs directly and immediately from the very nature of man. It is a right which a man or human being enjoys by virtue of the fact that he is a human person. It is the first of the fundamental rights of man deriving strictly from and based immediately on the dispositions of the natural law.

All rights and duties presuppose and are founded on existence. Once a person ceases to live or exist, everything else ceases. "Dead men don't bite is a famous and reasonable saying". Invariably, man's right to life, grounded in his divine origin, is the basis of all other human rights and foundation of a civilized society.

In support of this view, **Marshall** has noted that: "All human life, whatever its age, race, colour or creed, has equal value in the eyes of God; and must be accorded equal rights and treatment"(83). All human life is equal before God. This is the consequence of the fundamental natural equality of all men, in natural dignity.

There is therefore no man, no human authority, no science, no medical, social, economic or moral indication that can offer or produce a valid juridical title to a direct deliberate disposal of an innocent human life. The direct destruction of life whether born or unborn cannot in any way be justified.

Every life is worth preserving as long as God designs to sustain it. This principle is easily deduced from the fact that man is not the proprietor but the usufructuary of his life. Therefore, his life cannot be arbitrarily disposed of either by himself or by others.

All innocent lives are worth preserving. No one's right to life should be violated on the ground that such a person is less useful or useless, or a burden whether socially, politically or economically to the State. A person cannot be deprived of life on the ground that he is physically or mentally deficient.

Judged from this perspective, the incessant killing of people in the name of Boko Haram is scripturally and legally unacceptable. Such an act must be frowned upon and utterly relegated to the background.

Conclusion and Recommendations

The militant group, Boko Haram, whose violent struggle for an Islamic state in Northern Nigeria has killed thousands, has become the biggest threat to security in Africa. Their activities has not only attracted the attention of Nigerians, but has also attracted international outrage.

Nigeria and its neighbours say Boko Haram now threatens the security of the whole region. Cameroon has deployed armored vehicle and some 1,000 troops to its border region with Nigeria to counter the rising threat. In proffering solutions to the menace of Boko Haram, I recommend that we tackle it at three levels:

The Governmental Level

The Religious Level and

The Individual level.

We shall examine each of them:

Governmental Level

At the governmental level, the following should be done.

1.   Government should seek adequate advice and assistance from other countries that may have suffered terrorist attacks at one time or the other.

2.   Government should find out from those arrested what reasons they have for engaging in the fight and try to address such reasons.

3.   The traditional rulers and Emirs in the affected areas can also be called upon by government to make useful suggestions as to how the problem can be well handled.

4.   Government should find out who the sponsors of this sect are and take steps to punish them.

5.   The government must also ensure that the borders of Nigeria are well secured in order to prevent illegal entry and illegal exit. To ensure this, enough military personnel should be assigned to these places.

6.   The military should be equipped with more sophisticated weapons since the members of this sect themselves are well equipped.

7.   Government should ensure that religious tolerance is taught in schools and churches. With this, Muslims and Christians will be encouraged to tolerate one another.

8.   Government officials should ensure that jingles and adverts condemning   religious violence and riots are played on radio stations across the country.

9.   Vigilanty groups should also be encouraged by government in affected areas as they could help identify those who are members of this sect and consequently expose them to the wrath of the law.

Individual Level

At the individual level every person in the country is also expected to be security conscious and to report any strange movement or sinister activity to the law enforcement agents. At this point, everyone must be involved because if it does not affect you today, it will affect you tomorrow.

Religious Level

Prayer is a vital spiritual weapon for dealing with the menace of Boko Haram from its roots. This is significant because what is not dealt with from the root will always become an evil tree that will give birth to bitter fruit.

Since the country comprises basically Christians and Muslims, they need to pray earnestly that this menace be utterly eradicated. They need to pray for God to touch the heart of those who are perpetrators of this evil and cause them to repent of their sins and turn over a new leave.

Works Cited

Aneke, J. O. *Law for Everyman*. Ibadan: Intec Printers, 1987.

Ansaru. En. Wilkepedia.org/Wiki/Boko Haram. Retrieved 28/5/2014.

Boko Haram. "Ansaru Emerges". Vanguard Newspapers, 1 February 2013.

Criminal Code Act, Cap. 77, Laws of the Federation, 1990.

Graneris Giuseppe. *La Filosofia Del Diritto*. Roma: Editor Pontifici, 1961.

Igwe, Onyeka w. *Preliminary studies in human Rights law*. Lagos: Rings and Favolit, 2002.

Iwe, Nwachukwuike S. *The Inseparable Social Trinity: Religion, Morality and Law* Calabar: Saesprint, 2003.

Lubeck, Paul. *Muslim Societies*. London: Scott, 2009.

Marshall, J. *Medicine and Morals*. London: Longman, 1980.

Ngwodo, Chris. "Boko Haram Insurgency". www.Guardian.com News. 5 May, 2014. Retrieved 27 May, 2014.

Nyanya Bomb Blast – The Punch, 14 may, 2014

Oputa, C.A. *The Law and The Twin Pillars of Justice*. Owerri: Government Press, 1981.

Stamps, Donald C. *Life in Spirit Study Bible*. London: Zondervan, 1992

Uduigwomen, Andrew F. *A companion of Christian Philosophy*. Calabar: Ultimate Index, 2009.

Zenn, Jacob. *African Affairs*. London: Jamestown Foundation, 2013.

Journal of Integrative Humanism – Ghana: Vol. 4 No. 1, October, 2014, ISSN: 2026-6286

THE ROLE OF LANGUAGE IN THE ACQUISITION OF EDUCATION AND TECHNOLOGY: A CASE STUDY OF IGBO

BY

IWUCHUKWU, GODWIN CHINAEDU S.Ph.D
DEPARTMENT OF LINGUISTICS AND COMMUNICATION
STUDIES
UNIVERSITY OF CALABAR
goddyiwua@unical.edu.ng

ABSTRACT

The role of language especially; the mother tongue in development tends to be universally acknowledged by linguists. However, the extents to which this role can make or mar specific areas of development, in specific linguistic environments appear not to be fully appreciated. In this paper, selected students who are native speakers of Igbo language were taught technologically based subjects: Mathematics, Integrated Science and Introductory technology, in both English and Igbo, their mother tongue. At the end of the teaching period of two months, they were evaluated. The result shows that most of the students performed significantly better in each of the subjects taught in the mother tongue than in English. It is also discovered that they were more excited, interested and attentive when taught in their mother tongue than in English. This tends to suggest that Igbo native speakers acquire education and technology (aspects of development) faster in their mother tongue. It also suggests that their continued acquisition of these vital aspects of development (education and technology) in a language other than their mother tongue, will significantly mar their rate of acquisition and by extension their rate of development.

Resume: Le role de la langue, surtout celui de la langue maternelle dans le developpement est reconnu universellement par les linguistes. Cependant la mesure dans laquelle ce role peut encourager ou gener les domaines specifiques du developpement paraTt ne pasetre totalement appreciee Dans cette communiqué, trent eleves parlant Igbo comme langue maternelle ont ete enseignes des matieres a base technologigie a savior les Mathematiques, les Sciences et la technologie en anglais et en Igbo, leur langue maternelle. A la fin de I' enseignement qui a dure deux mois, ils ont ete evalues. Le resultat a montre que la plupart de ces eleves ont meuxtravaille dans chacune de ces matieres enseignees dans la langue maternelle qu'en anglais. II a ete aussi decouvert qu'ils etaient plus excites, interesses et attentifs lors de l'apprentissage en langue maternelle. Ceci suggere que ceux qui parlent Igbo comme leur langue maternelle acquerront l'education et al technologie (qui sont les aspects du developpement) plus rapidement s'ils sont enseignes dans la langue maternelle. II suggere aussi que l'acquisition de ces aspects important du developpement dans une autre langue que leur langue maternelle retardera le taux d'acquisition et par extension celui du developpement.

Key-words: *Language, Education, Mother Tongue, Technology, Igbo*

Introduction

In highlighting the role of language to the entire human existence, it has been define and as the "human essence" (Chomsky 1968) and as the "quit-essence of humanity" (Essien 1990:168). Every human being no matter their background makes use of language both positively and even negatively. It has also been acknowledged that language as a human essence comes through knowing a language well through acquisition and according to Essien (2005:6), the language one knows well is usually, the mother tongue. This means that the universally acclaimed role of language is not restricted only to develop widely used or international language but also to the smaller and local languages as long as they are well known to their speakers. Most African languages belong to this later category. The homogenizing effect of globalization according to Ejele (2004) has awakened dormant/nonchalant attitude and awareness of the importance of indigenous languages and mother tongues. The last decade witnessed a growing interest in the use of African languages in formal education as witnessed by the declaration of the year 1996 as the year of education in Africa. The aim of the declaration was to "foster new dynamism for education at the national and international levels" (ADEA, Newsletter 5). The Pan-African Seminar on the problems and prospects of the use of African languages in education held in Accra from August 26-30, 1996 also highlighted the advantages of using National languages in educating children and adult. The language component of Nigeria National Policy on education also recognizes the importance of these languages in education.

This work therefore, is aimed at highlighting the relevance of one of such African languages in education and technology acquisition. There has been several works of this nature relating to the language of instruction and the quality of the learner's performance. In a study on the cognitive level of statements made by Ghanaian pupils during discussions, cited in Nenty (1996), it was found that a lot more number of higher level cognitive statements were made using the mother tongue than English by these students. Fafunwa's Ife language project also revealed that education especially, at the primary level when given in the child's mother tongue rather than in a foreign language, is more effective and meaningful. Commenting on Fafunwa's work, Olarewaji (1991), said the study clearly indicated that the children taught the other subjects in Yoruba did significantly better academically than their counterparts who were taught in English. Yai (1976) reported of an experiment carried out in the teaching of the mother tongue using Fon language in the town of Cotonou in Catholic primary schools and this proved satisfactory. ADEA (1996) drew attention to the longitudinal study carried out by the center for minority education and research of the University of California, USA, involving Spanish-speaking students in schools across the states in the United States. The main conclusion of the study among others was "that the mother is the most effective language of instruction".

The present work provides a case study or data from another linguistic society, the Igbo, where the mother tongue plays a crucial role not only in education but also in the quest for technological advancement. Its uniqueness however, derives from the fact that it goes beyond the primary education where majority of such works were based to the junior secondary. It further reveals the implication of this to the technological backwardness of the Igbo and by extension, Nigeria and Africa.

Statement of the Problem/Purpose of Study:

There has been recently an outcry of the poor performance of Nigerian students especially, in science, mathematics and technical education in both the junior and senior certificate examinations conducted by two examination bodies (WAEC and NECO). Several reasons have been attributed to be responsible for this. Prominent among these reasons are those of Adesuyan (2006 and Nwokedi 1984). Adesuyan believes that the level of comprehension of spoken and written English is one of the major contributing factors to the poor performance of the students during examination, particularly in Mathematics for years. Adesuyan (2001:3) concludes that students no doubt understand Mathematics concept better if they are taught both in English and Nigeria languages". Nwokedi identifies a number of linguistic problems confronting the Nigeria child studying physics using English rather than his mother tongue. These range from linguistic ambiguities, complexities, grammatical error and lack of linguistic equivalent. While there appear to be no research proving the use of the second language to be more effective in the acquisition of education in general and technical education, in particular, the linguists of the exoglosic school of thought, however, point to the inadequate vocabulary repertoire of the most west African languages as a "credible" justification for the non relevant of this languages as media of instruction.

Given the fact that mathematics, science and technical education is a pivot to scientific advancement, the purpose of this study is therefore, to;

a. Discover the possibility of teaching Introductory Technology, Mathematics and Science in the junior secondary school, using Igbo as a medium;

b. Discover the significant rate of acquisition of students who are native speakers of Igbo on Mathematics, Introductory Technology and Integrated Science when taught in their mother tongue (Igbo);

c. Discover the significant rate of acquisition of student who are native speakers of Igbo on Mathematics, Introductory Technology and Integrated Science when taught in their second language (English).

d. Discover the attitudinal response of student who are native speakers of Igbo when they are taught in Integrative Science, Introductory technology, Mathematics in their mother tongue and their third language.

e. Discover the implication of the result of (a-d) to the quest for educational and technological advancement of the Igbo, Nigeria and Africa in general.

The Significant of the Study:

Apart from the Pan African Seminar on the problem and prospects on the use of African languages in education held in Accra from August 26-30th 1996 which highlighted the advantages of using National languages in educating children and adult, "the universal declaration of linguistics right (1996) endorsed the individuals with certain inalienable personal rights in language matters. According to Ememnanjo (2000), these includes, the rights to be recognized as a member of language community both in public and private, the rights for the individuals culture and language to be taught, the rights to interrelate and associate with other members of one's language community of origin, the rights to an equitable presence of one's language and culture in the communications media and the rights to receive attention in one's own language from government bodies and in socio-economic relations.

This study tends to highlight the possibility of teaching Mathematics, Science and Introductory technology subject even in the junior secondary school levels through the medium of the mother tongue. Its sensitizes speakers of the Igbo language of the inherent advantages in using their mother tongue for education and technology acquisition. Furthermore, it sensitizes every other users of the mother tongue of the inherent advantages in using the mother tongue for education and technology acquisition. Also, it seeks to raise the awareness of the mother tongue does not significantly influence their acquisition of education and technology.

Test of Hypothesis:

We have used the standard deviation as well as the pared t-test statistical instruments in the analysis of the assessments test as well as the hypothesis. The language of instruction is the independent variable while Igbo and English are the variant and covariate respectively. The decision role adopted is that which rejects the Null hypothesis (Ho) if t. calc is > t. tab.2.045 being our critical value. Ho is used for Null hypothesis. T. calc stands for t. calculated while t.tab stand for t. tabulated.

Assumption:

Our assumption is that the acquisition of these three subjects, Introductory Technology, Integrated Science and Mathematics is a good representation of acquisition technology and that the process of acquiring them is education.

Limitation:

One major constraint of this work is time. There could be an argument for a longer duration for the teaching than two months. This time constraint is a direct result of financial limitation. Such research project as this requires urge funding from UNESCO, NCOS, World Bank, Governments, etc, which has not come forth. What is however done here is to provoke and possibly attract such assistance for a larger skill research. This may thus be seen as a short term study which result may not significantly defer even when carried out for a longer time.

Analysis of Data:

Table 1: Assessment Test on Mathematics

Language of Instruction:	N	X	SD	t. calc.	t. tab
Igbo	30	51.067	13.455	4.62	2.045
English	30	40	18.242		

In table 1, t. calc > t. tab. The H_0 is rejected and the conclusion is that the mother tongue significantly influences the acquisition of mathematics. This further means that the student performed significantly better when they are taught mathematics in their mother tongue than when taught in English. The acquisition of mathematics tends to be significantly facilitated when it is done through the medium of the mother tongue. (It can also be said that the mother tongue can influence the acquisition of mathematics) in the junior secondary school which is our first hypothesis.

Table 2: Assessment Test on Introductory Technology

Language of Instruction:	N	X	SD	t. calc.	t. tab
Igbo	30	66.433	21.086	4.416	2.045
English	30	54.933	20.218		

In table 2, t. calc is > t. tab. The H_0 is rejected and the conclusion is that the mother tongue significantly influences their acquisition of Introductory Technology. The students performed significantly better when they are taught in English. The acquisition of introductory technology tends to be significantly facilitated when it is done through the medium of the mother tongue. This tends to validate the 2nd hypothesis that the mother tongue can influence the acquisition of introductory technology in the junior secondary school.

Table 3: Assessment Test on Integrated Science

Language of Instruction:	N	X	SD	t. calc.	t. tab
Igbo	30	71.5	17.655	9.530	2.045
English	30	55.3	18.775		

Using the same decision rule, since t. calc. is > t.tab, in Integrated Science, H_0 is rejected and this means that the mother tongue significantly influence their acquisition of Integrated Science. It further means that the students performed better when taught Integrated Science in Igbo than when taught in English.

The third hypothesis is also validated i.e. the mother tongue significantly influenced the acquisition of Integrated Science in the Junior Secondary School.

Table 4: Polled Values: Introductory Technology, Integrated Science and Mathematics.

Language of Instruction:	N	X	SD	t. calc.	t. tab
Igbo	90	63	19.538	9.530	2.045
English	90	50.078	20.195		

According to our decision rule, Ho is rejected because t. calc. is > t.tab in Mathematics, Introductory Technology and Integrated Science polled together. This means that the mother tongue significantly influence their acquisition of Introductory Technology, Integrated Science and Mathematics. It further means that students perform significantly better when taught Introductory Technology, Integrated Science and Mathematics in their mother tongue than when they are taught in English language. Having assumed that acquisition of Introductory Technology, Integrated Science and Mathematics is a reasonable measure of the acquisition of technology, education being the process of acquiring them, we can safely say that the mother tongue influence the acquisition of technology and education. The fourth hypothesis therefore, is upheld, i.e., the mother tongue significantly influences the acquisition of education and technology.

Summary of Findings:

From the analysis, it is discovered that the students performed significantly better, when they are taught mathematics in Igbo language (their mother tongue) than in English language, their second language. The same is the case for Integrated Science and Introductory Technology. In the polled value of the three subjects, it is discovered that t. calc is 9.530 while t. tab is 2.045. There is significant difference in performance in the mother tongue than in English language. In fact, the students' performance when taught in English is not significant. This suggests that the students have more understanding of the topics taught in the mother tongue. This findings agrees with Nwokedi and

Adesuyan's submission that English language creates a lot of ambiguity and difficulty in the students understanding of mathematics and physics and eventually, leads to their poor performance in them. Since acquiring mathematics, introductory technology and integrated science is a good representation of acquiring technology, this study reveals that English language posits an obstacle towards the easy and smote acquisition of education and technology by student who are native speakers of Igbo.

It is discovered again, that the students were more excited and interested to be taught mathematics, integrated science and introductory technology in their mother tongue than in English. They feel more at home as the mathematical, scientific and technical concepts and terms, which they could not readily understand in English are explain to them in their natural language. The significant role of the mother tongue is not only in the cognitive but also in the affective domains. Psychological, students were dull and unintelligent when English medium was used in teaching those subjects. When the mother tongue was used, they were interested, lively and creative (makes contributions and ask brilliant questions). This means that their thinking and thought processes are more challenged and provoked as they are taught in their mother tongue. Teaching them in their mother tongue therefore, tends to be the most appropriate way to task their mental capabilities and thinking scientifically. Teaching in English cannot guarantee these.

Scientific thinking is necessary for scientific and technological advancement of any people. Scientific and technological development and inventions are only possible when the people have begun to think scientifically. With the world wild web, the computer, the internet, information and communication, transfer or domestication of technology is easier when the people could think scientifically. This confirmed by Amfani (1998:2) who states that "the whole enterprise of scientific and technological advancement revolve around the ability to think scientifically". Acquiring education and technology by significant numbers of Igbo native speakers in English or a foreign language imposing certain constraints that hinder the manifestation of their fullest potentials and natural endowments. This has resulted to their underdevelopment and technological backwardness in the face of globalization. The case may not be different for all other linguistics societies acquiring education and technology in a foreign language, as some researches have already shown.

Some linguist have argued in favour of a few Igbo native speakers who have made some scientific land marks or others who have made some major scientific break through using a second or foreign language such as English. The point however, is that in education and technological acquisition, exceptional person who could not make a mark in whatever language given to them, cannot suffice as referent point. The majority or a significant number of the people should be the most rational referent points. For example, in the individuals analysis of the performance of each of the 30 students taught, and average of 1-5 (3-16%) performed better when taught Mathematics, Introductory Technology and Integrated Science in English than Igbo. Some of them performed better in English in one or two out of three subjects. By our analysis and assumption; it means that this percentage acquire education and technology better in the second language (English than their mother tongue). Furthermore, this same percentage are more interested and excited when taught in the second language. On the other hand, 25 of the student in bracket 84% add significant improvement and performed better than when taught in their mother tongue. This same number of students enjoys and understands the teaching more in the mother tongue. Such statistic leaves no empirical bases for the preference of the second language as the medium of acquisition of education and technology more than the mother tongue. No other continent in the world has developed or attempted to develop with a foreign language except Africa and she is paying daily for it.

Recommendation:

In the light of the findings of this study, we make the following recommendations:

1. Adoption of the mother tongue or the language of the immediate community as the language of basic education (as in Nigeria's UBE programme) and senior secondary school.

2. Mass production of Igbo (Other West African languages) teachers from the colleges of education and faculties of education in our universities with language and science combination as Chemistry/Igbo, Igbo/Physics, Igbo/Mathematics, etc.

3. The inclusion of the use of West African languages in education and technology acquisition as one of the targets to be realized in the millennium development goals (MDG).

4. A credit pass in West Africa languages should be considers along side with English as a pre-condition for admission into tertiary institution.

Conclusion:

The findings of this study as shown that the Igbo native speakers acquire education and technology faster in their mother tongue than in English. There is a significant difference in their rate of acquisition of education and technology in their mother tongue (Igbo) than in English. The acquisition of education and technology by Igbo native speakers in English has adverse influence not only on their cognitive performance but also psychologically. Their continued acquisition of education and technology (aspects of development) in the language other than their mother tongue, will significantly mare their rate of acquisition and by extension their rate of development. Igbo and other West African languages should not only be the medium of pedagogical instructions from the primary to the secondary, but their use in education must be entrench as part of the millennium development goals. A linguistics reform tends to be one sure way of avoiding the escalation of the crisis of technological underdevelopment of the African continents.

References:

Adesuyan, A. "Nigerian Languages and Mathematics education". Paper presented at the Annual Conference of the Association of Nigeria Languages Teachers. Aba. NINLAN, 2001.

ADEA. Association for the Development of Education in Africa, News Letter. 1996.

Amfani, A. "Nigerian Language in Scientific and Technological Advancement: A case Study of Hausa". Paper presented at the Annual Conference of the Association of Nigeria Languages Teachers. Usman Dan Fodio University 1998, 1-6.

Chomsky, Noam. Language and the mind. New York: Harcourt Brace and World Inc. 1968.

Essien, Okon. "The future of minority languages" Multilingualism Minority Language Policy in Nigeria. Ed. Emenangjo, Nolue. Agbor: C.B.L, 1990.

Ejele, Philomena. The Challenges of Linguistic and Cultural Diversities. The Heritage of Humanity: Insights from the Nigerian Experience. A lead paper presented at the Prof. Okon, Essien at 60 symposium. 25-27th May, 2004. University of Calabar of Calabar.

Ememnanjo, N. "The Language Situation in Nigeria". Journal of Education for National Development and International Co-operation 4:1:18-35, 2000.

Essien, Okon. Language and the Nigerian Reforms Agenda. A Keynote Address Delivered at the 19th conference of the Linguistic Association of Nigeria held at the University of Nigeria, Nsukka 25-28th Sept, 2005.

Nenty, Johnson. "Relative Influence of Language on Primary and secondary school pulpils' performance in science and mathematics in Lesotho". JOSARAMSE: 31-35-49, 1996.

Nwokedi, R. "Language problems in Teaching and Learning Science in Nigeria: Physics". The Nigerian Language Teacher 6:1, 8-16, 1984.

Iwuchukwu, Godwin. "Teaching Metalanguage as a part of Igbo L, Curriculum". Paper presented at the symposium on the 66 Birthday Anniversary of Prof. Okon, Essien, University of Calabar. 25-27th May, 2004.

Olarewaju, A. "The Potency of Yoruba as a Medium for teaching and Learning Science and Learning in Nigerian Languages. Ed Egbe Ehiametalor. Lagos: Okanlawon, 1991:93-98.

Yai, O. "Language and Education in Dahomey" Mother Tongue in Education the West African Experience. Ed. Bamglose Ayo. Paris: UNESCO, 1996. 63-83.

Journal of Integrative Humanism – Ghana: Vol. 4 No. 1, October, 2014, ISSN: 2026-6286

UNDERSTANDING EMPOWERMENT FOR SUSTAINABLE DEVELOPMENT IN NIGERIA: A THEATRE AND PARTICIPATORY COMMUNICATION APPROACH

BY

*ADIE EDWARD UGBADA & **AFO DONALDSON USHIE
DEPARTMENT OF THEATRE AND MEDIA STUDIES
UNIVERSITY OF CALABAR, CALABAR – NIGERIA
*eddytorial@yahoo.com, **donaldsonushie@gmail.com

ABSTRACT

The term "Empowerment" has been in use for a very long time. It is a common term used by various governments and non-governmental organizations (NGOs) to mean the act of helping the poor in society. In Nigeria, governments and NGOs have embarked on different programmes which are said to be empowering the poor. However, instead of achieving development through these professed empowerment programmes, the poor in Nigeria have remained un-empowered and impoverished the more as sixty- five per cent of Nigerians cannot afford descent two-square meals in a day. The poor have on the contrary become more dependent on government and NGOs. The various monies and gift-sharing occasions from government and NGOs to the poor have not translated into sustainable empowerment as it were. The very few poor who have benefited from the so-called empowerment programmes eventually have nothing to show for it after a short while. This is due to the fact that the so-called empowerment is not sustainable and people cannot grow or get empowered when the enabling socio-political and economic atmosphere is not in place. This paper therefore, argues that the money and gift-sharing empowerment programmes of government and NGOs cannot be sustainable and therefore could lead the poor into more hardship as they become more dependent. This paper attempts to discuss what empowerment is and what it is not vis –a vis the place of theatre in achieving empowerment.

Key-Words: *Empowerment, Sustainable Development, Theatre, Participatory Communication*

Introduction

Certain human situations bring about the idea of empowering poor people. These situations are actually unpleasant and undesirable state of being for male and female in society. Therefore, there is no gainsaying that the idea of empowerment in whatever form it takes has been in existence since civility when man began to look for ways to improve the lots of society. These undesirable situations range from poverty, illiteracy, diseases, inimical cultural beliefs and practices, gender inequality and the likes which have brought untold hardship on the human being.

Human undesirable conditions could be caused by man-made factors as mentioned above and natural factors such as weather, climate, natural disasters like earthquakes, tsunami, flood etc. In this vein, efforts have been taken by governments and NGOs to alleviate these undesirable human conditions.

Poverty for example, may be caused by the human being by being lazy or careless and illiteracy is also an inducer of poverty in modern times. Natural disaster, war or insurgency can also destroy the means of livelihood of people. Gender inequality and certain cultural beliefs have also caused poverty and diseases in so many parts of the world and the very evident example can be found in the northern parts of Nigeria where many children (most especially female) do not go to school and the girl child is forced into early marriage, become diseases prone and remain dependent on their husbands. Cultural and religious beliefs which do not allow women in public can also be a road map to poverty and dependency amongst women thereby giving men the moral superiority over them. All these strengthen the menace of gender inequality and chauvinism in society.

The implication of the above hypothesis is that more women are oppressed, poor, dependent and disease prone and these undesirable conditions have brought to the fore the issue of empowerment by governments and NGOs in Nigeria.

Misconception of the Term Empowerment in Nigeria

The issue of poverty, disease, illiteracy and other societal problems are caused by what constitute a society itself. It is said that a doctor cannot cure a disease without identifying and eliminating the causative agent. It is in the same way that a people cannot be empowered or developed without identifying and fighting the factors that disempower them. Freire (1972) posits that:

> In order to determine whether a society is developing, one must go beyond criteria based on indices of per capital income which expressed in statistical form, are misleading as well as those which concentrate on the study of gross income. The basic elementary criterion is whether or not the society (people and environment) is a being for itself.

This simply translates that the political, economic and cultural decision-making power must reside and locate within the people.

In the light of the above, governments and NGOs who claim to be empowering people are simply working on the surface. Governments have most often tried to solve problems without finding out the cause of such problems. This is so because such problems of society are caused by either commissions or omissions of people in government and example of such omissions or commissions are the very evident corrupt practices which have eaten up every strata of government business. Therefore, it makes ridiculous any attempt of governments or NGOs to be sharing gifts and money to people in the name of empowerment and development. This approach is like postponing the evil days because people are merely given fish and not being taught how to fish. But empowerment could mean teaching people how to catch fish for themselves.

Strands of Misconceived Empowerment Programmes

The Gombe State Ministry of Women Affairs, according to the Nation Newspaper (Tuesday July 21, 2009) spent the sum of twenty- nine million, five hundred thousand naira (29,500,000) to build what it called Girl-Child Centre and Orphanage. This gesture is necessary but the questions to ask are, has the ministry taught it wise to do a research into the root causes of problem facing the girl-child and dumped babies? Has the ministry thought of measures to fight the root causes of the menace?

The Kaduna State Government under the leadership of then governor Arc. Namadi Sambo distributed cars and motorcycles to unemployed youths as means of empowerment as reported by Nigerian Television Authority (NTA) Network News (15th Nov. 2009). It is important to interrogate the criteria used to arrive at who benefited and who did not and to imagine how many unemployed youths will the Kaduna State Government continue to give cars and motorcycles. It was discovered that not long after this government gesture, many youths hit the roads with their motorcycles and cars and this increased the rate at which accident occurred leading to environmental hazards.

The National Agency for Poverty Eradication programme (NAPEP), which was established under the administration of former President Olusegun Obasanjo has in many ways involved itself in the business of empowerment and one of its contributions is the distribution of tricycles and motorcycles to many youths to enable them engage in commercial transportation in order to make a living out of it. It was observed that at that time the beneficiaries of these tricycles soon ran into troubles with their machines which developed faults and their spare parts were very expensive beyond what they could afford which eventually led to the abandonment of the machines. The AM Express programme of the NTA on (23rd Nov. 2009) brought to the notice of the public the problematic nature of the tricycles showing the beneficiaries lamenting over their ordeals and how most of them had no jobs to do after abandoning their tricycles. Again, this brings to the questioning of what empowerment really means.

At the end of most of these empowerment programmes, little or nothing is added to the socio-political and economic environment of the people. It rather created an atmosphere of dependency on government interventions.

Understanding Empowerment

The concept 'Empowerment' may have been interpreted in several varying ways by development experts or agents. However, it is conceptually wrong when a body or people think they have the monopoly for development. Nobody is an expert when issues of development are discussed; rather, everyone is involved through dialogue. Freire (1972) observed that "nobody knows all and nobody knows nothing". Therefore, development and empowerment cannot be handed over from one person to the other. It has to involve a holistic process through the involvement of people. Every means of empowerment and development should be identifiable, acceptable and the people should have sense of ownership of the process to endanger sustainability. According to Bergall (1993), empowerment suggests a very important qualitative dimension of participatory approaches which bring about self-reliance. Guijt and Meera (1998), described empowerment from the point that it is about the people gaining the ability to undertake activities, set their own agenda and change events. This position of Guijt and Meera simply refer to a way of involving people actively in decision-making process. It involves developing confidence in people's capacity which enables them to understand the reality of their situation, reflect on the factor shaping that situation and most critically, take steps to effect changes or improve on it.

The concept of empowerment should not be misconceived as even the Longman Dictionary of Contemporary English defines empowerment as "to give someone more control over his life or situation and to give an organization the power or legal right to do something. Empowerment is not meant for those who have power already such as the rich and powerful in society. The focus of empowerment is basically for the poor, oppressed, neglected and the masses in general. The process of empowerment makes the individual or group of individuals perceive themselves and their ability to influence their environment around them. It is important to note that empowerment of people goes beyond a mere participation of the people. Empowerment according to Brook (1972) is a multi-dimensional process involving the transformation of the economic, social, psychological, political and legal circumstances of the powerless in society. By implication therefore, an empowerment focus involves a holistic and sincere radical alteration of the structures which reproduce the subordinate position of the powerless. Simply put, there should be a dismantling of status quo such as norms, traditional practices, injustices, chauvinism, rigging and hegemonic tendencies in general because all these disempower and dispossess the powerless.

It is obvious that in the different but correlating definitions of empowerment, there is one emphatic and common denominator. This denominator is the essence of people's participation in decision-making and setting agenda. Chris (2008) opines that the people must have control of their economic, political and psychological environment.

It is important to note that the term empowerment cannot be disconnected from the term power. It takes an individual or a collective power to empower people. Either individual or collective, empowerment cannot take place if in the first place; those involved don't have power (knowledge, participation and ability to help themselves).

According to Melkote and Steeves (2001), for empowerment to take place, people should have power to generate new possibilities without domination, power with the people (collective) which is created by group process and power from within which strengthens, inspires and energizes people to be able to do something. They argued further that "real change (empowerment) may not be possible unless we address power iniquities between marginalized individuals and groups at the grass root and those who make policy and aid decisions". Steeves' and Melkote's position, simply articulated, means that power from within is important in any empowerment process so that the poor can have power and control over their situations. This is unlike the Nigerian situation in which NGOs and GOs claim to empower people without their adequate involvement in the process of the empowerment strategies. Empowerment should be a collective process whereby the poor's consciousness and confidence are built in order for them to be able to fight those things that oppress them. Melkote and Steeves (2001) again, define empowerment as the process by which individuals, organizations and communities gain control and mastery over social and economic conditions. Guijt and Meera (1998) describe empowerment succinctly thus:

> Empowerment is about people gaining the ability to undertake activities, to set their own agenda and change events. This interpretation is based on the traditional model of power and may simply involve giving people an active role in a decision-making process... it implies enabling people to understand the reality of their situation, reflect on the factors shaping that situation and most critically take steps to effect changes to improve it... as a result, it must include processes that lead the individual or group to perceive itself as able to occupy a decision making pace.

They argued further that a genuine empowerment process should collectively (with the less privileged) ask the following questions:

1. What are the problems to be tackled?
2. Why do the problems exist?
3. How can we bring about change?

In the light of the definitions of empowerment above, it is clear that the empowerment claims or strands by GOs and NGOs in Nigeria are not in the real sense empowering. Power and gender inequalities, cultural factors and the causes of the undesirable human conditions as well as collective participation in solving problems in a sustainable way must be put into adequate consideration and analysis by development agents.

Participation, Gender Analysis and Empowerment

Guijt and Meera (1998) posit that:

> The cutting edge of development practice in the 1990s up until now is described in terms of 'participation', 'community-driven action' and 'empowerment'. The broad aim of participatory development is to increase the involvement of socially and economically marginalized people in decision making over their own lives. The assumption is that participatory approaches empower local people with the skills and confidence to analyze their situation, reach consensus, make decisions and take action so as to improve their circumstances. The ultimate goal is more equitable and sustainable development.

121

As earlier stated in this paper, empowerment is multi-dimensional and many scholars who have written on it have opined that there can be no holistic empowerment programme if the issue of gender is not given adequate consideration. Halfani observes that empowerment without a woman is incomplete and insincere. He defines women empowerment as the positive change of the economic, social, psychological, political and legal situations of women in the society. He argued further that women empowerment goes beyond only positive changes in the mentioned critical aspect but also the demolition of cultural norms, traditional practices, hegemonic and religious doctrine that relegate women to the background.

Women empowerment entails the expansion of women's access to educational opportunities, skills acquisition and allowance to occupy political and economic authorities. The involvement of women in all cultural, political and economic issues of a country simply emphasizes women's participation like their male counterparts. This study further submits that women empowerment should entail the demolition of power relation between genders in the distribution of societal resources which has hitherto been favouring men.

A lot of societies have not been able to experience growth in Nigeria (mostly in the north) because many women are restricted from public services, expression, participation and even education. On the contrary, women empowerment should advocate opportunities for women to develop their talents, get their enablement to contribute meaningfully to societal development as women empowerment translate into improved lives of children. Griffen (1989) argued that empowerment is adding to women's power.

The struggles of women activists all over the globe has made it compelling to enhance the status of women and making the issue gaining recognition in recent times. Beijing China hosted in September 1995 a Fourth World Conference on women and the themes were equality, development and peace. The conference articulated strategies to attain women empowerment in the globe. These strategies are meant to fight the following:

1. Violence against women.
2. The persistent and increasing burden of poverty on women.
3. Inequalities and inadequacies in and unequal access to health care and related services.
4. The effect of armed or other kinds of conflict on women including those living under foreign occupation.

5. Gender inequalities in the management of natural resources and in the safeguarding of the environment.
6. Persistent discrimination against and violation of the right of the girl child.
7. Lack of respect for and inadequate promotion and protection of the human rights of women.
8. Stereotyping of women and inequality in women's access to and participation in all communication systems, especially in the media.
9. Inequality between men and women in the sharing of power and decision making at all levels.
10. Insufficient mechanism at all levels to promote the advancement of women.
11. Inequalities in economic structures and policies in all forms of productive activities and in access to resources.

These articulated strategies of a global conference underscore the importance of women empowerment for national and global development. Therefore, this study recommends that the above strategies should be put into use in Nigeria for the purpose of rapid socio-economic and political environment. Government and NGOS should support these strategies for a holistic rural-urban development.

Gender analysis is very vital in carrying out a successful empowerment programme but agents of development had always got the problem in doing this. This is due to the fact that there are misconceptions in perspectives of development agents as they ignorantly address the issue of gender as a mere male prejudice against women and have used this idea to work towards the liberation of women through empowerment. Irene and Meerah (1998) observe thus:

> In most development intervention sectors, gender is taken to mean women and women are treated as an identifiable single category, thought of in a new narrow range of stereotypical race. They argued further that gender analysis in most cases do not extend to the analysis of men's position in development interventions and in this light, this study advocates the consideration of the peculiarities of both sexes in gender analysis for empowerment in order to achieve balanced participation.

Cornwall (2003) puts it like this:

Disregarding the complexity of difference doesn't help anymore, least of all those whose livelihoods are at stake in development interventions. Making assumptions about people based on their sex does not get us anywhere in working with them.

The above position is correct because there are men who are even more oppressed in society than women. There are men who are marginalized and subjected to the brutality of prejudice because they couldn't achieve what a man supposedly should achieve.

The argument of this research therefore suggests that in gender analysis for development, the issues should not merely end at the sex but every sex category of people who participatorily contribute towards development. For example, if women are to be considered in the polity, the questions to ask are:

a. Who are the women?
b. What class of women?
c. Are the poor women parts of it?

The same questions are to be asked if we are considering men too. Irene and Meerah (1998) declare thus:

It is crucial that facilitators take a step back and reflect on their own preconceived ideas and prejudices. By working with the differences affect local people's lives and livelihood, rather than with blanket notions of differences that fail to do justice to the complexities of most people's lived realities, they can then take a step forward to work effectively for change.

This research advocates that development agents or facilitators should not in their gender analysis procedures create a battle ground on which other accusations are made. Gender analysis deals with all-women, men, old, young, boys, girls for balanced participation and sustainable empowerment.

Theatre as Tool for Empowerment

Theatre has the capacity to bring people together, engage them in a pedagogic and learning process. Theatre for Development (TFD) is a veritable tool through which Participatory Communication can be achieved for the purpose of effective orientation of people (the poor in particular) towards the betterment of their lives. Theatre for Development (TFD) is an experimental form of theatre which is radical and unconventional when compared with other forms of theatre. TFD as a theatre form is evolving and its last word has not been said due to its unending nature Osofisan (2004:18), Kidd (1978:42) argued that Theatre for Development as Development Communication advocates people's participation and self-reliance in their developmental process. According to Okwori:

> One method that has continued to lend itself amenable to participation is Popular Theatre. It has an inbuilt mechanism for involving people; for discussing strategies for survival; for enabling people to rediscover their potentials and capacity in a non-intimidating manner. By definition and intention therefore, TFD subscribes to the tenets of Participatory Action Research (PAR) (2002:160).

Okwori further argued that TFD has the following participatory capabilities.

i.   Its entertainment qualities give it the capacity to attract and hold the interest of large number of people

ii. As an oral medium done in the language of the people, it involves ordinary people who are often excluded from development initiations.

iii. In dramatically representing local problems, it provides a codification of reality which can be used by participants in analyzing their situations.

Theatre for Development intervention passes through different stages. Okwori (2004) describes TFD process to begin from choosing the location or target of the intervention and the consultation with the community leaders who are also described as gatekeepers in order to seek permission from them to carry out an intervention. This stage is called the familiarization stage. This is important because it creates an environment of mutual understanding between the outsiders and the insiders (development agents and community people) towards achieving a common goal. This stage also allows for familiarity with the community based groups whose contributions will be highly useful in the exercise. The next stage deals with community research which is carried out by both the outsiders and the insiders over issues affecting the community. In this stage, TFD tools such as Participatory Action Research (PAR) Participatory Learning and Action (PLA) Participatory Communication (PC) and many others are adopted in the process of research. This stage leads to the gathering of information and data (findings). These findings are therefore analyzed in a participatory way by all and prioritization is done over the numerous issues that would have emerged. This process of analysis which is participatory is in itself empowering as knowledge is shared amongst the locals and the outsiders.

This stage also allows for suggested solutions to problems to be examined and therefore, one of the ways that transformative learning can take place is the stage of play creation over the issues which are enacted and presented to the general audience. The stage of presentation in Theatre for Development as a process for communication is a very crucial and much expected one. This is because the performance stage is the crux of TFD exercise in which subject, thoughts, issues are interrogated and solutions are proffered to existing problems in a play way. This means that the locals of the community are participants as they play roles in the research, data analysis, prioritizing of issues up to the presentation. (Okwori 2002:169) In this way, lessons, morals (didactic) are collectively drawn in a participatory communication model. The performance in TFD creates avenues for dialogical communication, argument and counter argument as well as interrogation for clarification of grey issues about the people's realities of life. The collective play creation process brings to the fore the careful evaluation of solutions out of issues or problems identified. This allows for action plans by the participants towards solving observed problems.TFD conforms with the agreement that the communicative act is not the mere transfer of meaning, but the achievement of a parallel in the structure of internal meaning, the responses of both communicators as receivers so that the meaning remains in the behavioural system or cognitive structure of the respective parties Olowu (1989:68).

Conclusion

World over, there exist undesirable conditions which warrant that those in position of power who are privileged empower the less-privileged or the poor for balanced societal growth and development in a sustainable way. However, empowerment programmes in Africa and Nigeria in particular have not been approached in a way that society can regenerate itself and the less-privileged being able to sustain growth. In this light therefore, this paper concludes that for effective and sustainable empowerment of the less-privilege in Nigeria, there is the need for the consideration of factors such as participation, balanced gender analysis, cultural factors in the process of identifying the causes of the undesirable conditions and how they can be collectively tackled with a view to achieving sustainable empowerment. This paper further posits that theatre can go a long way in engaging people for their empowerment.

References

Cornwall, A. and Pratt, G. *Pathways to Participation.* Southampton Row, London. ITDG Pub. 2003.

Chris, M. and Ruth, F. (2008) *Challenges of Popular Participation to Policy Implementation in Nigeria: Case Study of Rural Poverty Alleviation.* 41-45 of Journal of Gombe State University. Vol. 1

Freire, P. *Pedagogy of the oppressed.* New York, Seabury (1970).

Guijt, I. and Shah, M. (eds) (1998) *The Myth of Community.* London, ITDG Pub.

Irene, G. and Meera, K. (ed.) (1998) *The Myth of Community.* ITDG Pub. 103-105 Southampton Row, London WUB HHL. UK

Kamzer, M. (1957) *Contemporary Psychoanalytic Views of Aesthetics.* Psychoan Asso. London

Longman Dictionary of Contemporary English, New Edition

Melkote, S. ans Steeves, L. (2001) *Communication for Development in the Third World.* London, Sage Pub.

Nigerian Television Authority Network News. (15th Nov. 2009)

Nigerian Television Authority AM Express Programme on the 23rd Nov. 2009.

Osita, E. (2008) *Women Economic Empowerment and Nigerian Drama in Femi Osofisan International Journal.* Paper 184, Valid Pub: Awka

Okwori, J. (1992) *Popular Theatre, Popular Participation and Empowerment in Women Digest.* Vol. 5

Richard, C. (1974) *Play, Drama and Thought.* Drama Book. Specialist New York.

Ralf, A. (ed.) (2008) *Contemporary Issues in Mass Media for Development and National Security.* Malthouse Press ltd, Lagos.

Remi, A. and Francis, E. (ed.) (1999) *Elements of Politics.* Sam Iroanusi Pub. Lagos

Srinivas, R. and Leslie, S. (2001) *Communication for Development in the Third World.* Sage Publications: New Delhi, London.

The Nation Newspaper (July 21, 2009) Gombe State Women Ministry Spends 29.5 Million for Girl-Child Centres

Thomas, J. and Jan, S. (ed.) (1999) *Theoretical Approaches to participatory Communication.* Hampton Press, Inc. Cresskill, New Jersey

Journal of Integrative Humanism – Ghana: Vol. 4 No. 1, October, 2014, ISSN: 2026-6286

EVIDENCE OF SOCIAL INEQUALITY IN IGBO PROVERBS
BY

*IWUCHUKWU, GODWIN C.S. Ph.D & **NDIMELE, ROSELINE I. Ph.D

***DEPARTMENT OF LINGUISTICS AND COMMUNICATION STUDIES.
UNIVERSITY OF CALABAR, CALABAR..
**DEPARTMENT OF LINGUISTICS AND COMMUNICATION/IGBO
ABIA STATE UNIVERSITY, UTURU
*godwiniwuchukwu@yahoo.com, **ihumele@yahoo.com**

ABSTRACT

Chinua Achebe in his much celebrated novel, **Things Fall Apart** gave a good insight into the definition and role of proverbs in Igbo culture when he said "proverb is the oil with which they eat words". More recent studies of Igbo proverbs tend to show that Achebe's statement on Igbo proverbs though insightful and a pioneering one, being one of the earliest formal definitions on the subject, is limited as a definition and restricted in function. This paper focuses on Igbo proverbs with a view to uncovering its additional roles in the Igbo socio-cultural as well as linguistic environment which may lead to the expansion of its definition and function. Using a number of Igbo proverbs with their apt descriptions and usage in the society, it is discovered that the mastery and competence on the use of proverbs confers certain linguistic cum literary privileges that pedestals them as **unequal** with those that have less or no mastery and competence in the use of proverbs. It is discovered that this linguistic cum literary inequality ultimately translates to a kind of social inequality. The paper further avers that in the contact between English and African Languages such as Igbo, this phenomena have equally influenced the evaluation and perception of African writers in Igbo and or African (Igbo) writers in English. Our conclusion is that proverbs in Igbo language provide a significant evidence for the determination of Hudson's (1980:5) subjective linguistic inequality which translates to social inequality.

Key-words: *Proverbs, Social Inequality, Igbo, Linguistic Inequality, Linquistic Equality*

Introduction

Research on proverbs has been enormous and extensive, whether proverbs in Igbo or proverbs in other language and socio-cultural groups. In

128

fact, proverb can be said to be one of the sociolinguistic phenomena universal in all languages even though this is not captured in Chomsky's description of language universal in his grammatical theory. Obviously, this tend to be because of his disdain for the inclusion of language use (sociolinguistics) in the analysis of linguistic competence. Adeiyongo (2004:253) citing Ridout and Witting (1967) had commented on the long history of proverb in the classroom as early as the 10th century when proverbs were used in England as a brighter method of teaching Latin. According to him, the commonest proverbs still form part of the background of every English speaking child, and this is recognized in the early stages of modern education, where many and varied uses are made of them. He further pointed out that many generations of children through the 19th century and beyond were expected to improve their minds as well as their writings by having to copy proverbs out in their copy-books.

Finnegan (1970) had shown that among some societies in Africa, proverbs could be used by an individual for 'comment for persuasion' in an esoteric manner so that it could either deliberately convey ambiguity or only very few people could understand him. Raum in Adeiyongo (2004:254) further posits that among the east Africans,

> From fourteen when a child flies into rage, when he
> is recalcitrant or violates the code of etiquette, when
> he makes an ass out of himself, when he is cowardly,
> he hears his actions commented upon in the words of
> a proverb.

He believes that such a comment is meant to correct the child so that he could not repeat such a thing the next time as the proverb would have a lasting effect on him. Ashipu (2006:127) reveals that African proverbs constitute a rhetorical form which offers the speaker and the philosopher a veritable medium for the projection and fulfillment of a variety of socially desired goals. He continued to state that wherever there is doubt about an accepted pattern of behavior, stipulated line of action, traditional norms are threatened; there is always proverbs to couch, illuminate and buttress the wisdom of the traditional code of conduct. Ashipu agrees with the universality of the existence and function of proverbs across languages and cultures when he shows what proverb is and means to various societies. According to him, the Bosman believes that proverbs in conversation are torches in darkness. For the

Persians, proverbs are the adornment of speech and the Romans assert that proverbs are salt-pits from which you may extract salt and sprinkle it where you will. For the Igbo proverbs are the palm oil with which words are eaten, and to the Yoruba, proverb is the vehicle of conversation, when the conversation drops, the proverb revives it. To the Hausa, the proverb is the beginning of words which are taken and fumbled up that a man may not know their meanings. The TIV believe that the most valuable legacy a man can bequeath to a child to enable such a child steer his way through life is not corporal but is terms of instruction in proverbs.

Mele (2006.4) shows how proverbs can be used to resolve conflicts across the language groups and cultures that use them. This he illustrated with four proverbs from four different language groups as presented below. The proverbs were all translated into English. The language groups are Lesotho, Igbo, Zulu and Hausa.

(a) A fright between grasshoppers is a joy to the crow (Lesotho).
(b) When the brother's fight to the death, a stranger inherits their father's state- (Ibo) sic (Igbo).
(c) He who hates, hates himself (Zulu)
(d) He that forgives gains the victory (Hausa)

His argument is that such proverbs can be used to broker peace, love, and hospitality among the warring groups in the various societies.

Most of these works on proverbs have not projected proverb as revealing clear linguistic inequality that translates to social inequality which is the central focus of this paper. Though many linguists do not subscribe to the notion of linguistic inequality, but drawing from a number of Igbo proverbs, this research tend to show that linguistic inequality encapsulated in proverbs, clearly exist in Igbo. We will further show how this translates to social inequality. The implication of this is the need for the adjustment of the restricted definition and function of Igbo proverbs to accommodate the emerging role.

Linguistic Equality VS Linguistic Inequality

According to Hudson (1980:205), linguistic equality postulated by most linguists exists at the level of language structure. On the other hand, linguistic inequality postulated more by non-linguists exist at the level of language use. Structurally, most linguists tend to agree that no language is superior to the other no matter the size of its speakers or the level of its development. This implies that even when a language is not yet described to the point of having orthography or writing system, it still possesses certain rules that govern its operation in for example. Affixation and word formation processes, phrasal categorizations, sentence constructions, articulator process pattern and other phonetic / phonological rule operations. It is in this respect that Chomsky has come up with his universal Grammar (UG) which we describe here as not only an attempt to showcase the unity in diversity among grammatical systems but also the structural equality of the systems. According to Uoene (2007:164) a language universal is that every language sound system is made up of significant consonants and vowels. They are significant in that they allow for the discriminate of meanings in collocation with other sounds.

There is no purely linguistic basis to code between the grammars of two completely different and unfamiliar language varieties one considered standard and high variety and another non–standard and low variety.

Linguists like Hudson recognize the existence of linguistic inequality which according to him exists at the level of language use but not at level of structure. In fact he recognizes three types of linguistic inequality which include: subjective linguistic inequality, strictly linguistic inequality and communicative inequality. Communicative inequality is concerned with knowledge of how to use linguistic items to communicate successfully instead of just knowing the items. Strictly linguistic inequality as maintained by Hudson relates to the linguistic items that a person knows since the items that one knows reflect the experience one has had, and that people with different experiences know different ranges of items. Subjective inequality concerns what people think about each other's speech. For some societies people are credited with different amounts of intelligence, friendliness and other such virtues according to the way they speak, evidence from the Igbo society through her proverbs to buttress the authenticity of Hudson linguistic inequality. The evidence from Igbo proverbs could well be relevant in the three types of his inequality especially the subjective inequality.

Restricted Definition and Function Vs Expanded Definition of Igbo Proverbs

Chinua Achebe is his much celebrated novel, "Things Fall Apart" gave a good insight into the definition and role of proverbs in Igbo culture when he said "proverbs are the palm oil with which words are eaten Achebe (1958:5). Achebe's statement on Igbo proverbs though insightful and a pioneering one, being one of the earliest formal definitions on the subject, is limited as a definition and restricted in function knowing that Achebe was neither writing an essay nor dissertation on Igbo proverbs, our categorization of its limitedness in definition and restriction in function is the fact it tend to address only what proverb does in conversation and speech. It garnishes and embellishes both the oral and written expressions of the Igbo native speaker as well as considered a very necessary component of such expression. However, there tend to be a concealment of other aspects of the definition and function. For example, Bhuvareswar (2004)'s definition of proverbs as,

> The most popular figurative expression. A concise familiar phrase or sentence in a given language (Igbo) that contains advice about life, which can serve as a commentary on social practices of a people. It contains folk wisdom, with culture specific generalizations arrived at after observing a particular social practice.

The above definition applies to Igbo proverbs. It goes beyond decorating speech, but contains advice of Igbo people. To comment and criticize the wasteful expenditure lifestyle of a prodigal child or student, the proverbs given below can be employed.

Igbo Prov.:   "Nwa akwo n'azu amaghi na ije na ara ahu"

Gloss: The child carried at the back, does not know that trekking is a difficult exercise.

Comment: A child or students whose school fees is paid by the parents does not know the suffering they undergo to do so. That is why the child can want and spend money recklessly.

Igbo prov: Otu mkpisiaka ruta mmanu o zuo oha.

Gloss: When one finger touches palm oil, it spreads to other fingers.

Comment: When someone joins his friend to do what is wrong e.g. stealing without asking him to stop when the friend is caught, the punishment that will be meted to the thief will extend to him.

The Igbo proverbs such as the ones above not only contain advice about life but also comments on the social practices of the people. Furthermore, a number of researches have shown the various functions of proverbs which also applies to Igbo proverbs which tend not to be captured in Achebe's statement. Mele (2006:2) states that proverbs safeguard a society's way of life by preserving material, social and ideological aspects of a culture, teach diversity of cultures indispensable for the human species to thrive on. It serves as rationalizations of reflective observations of social life, human values and natural phenomena and as well reveal distinctive world views of the different societies. Specifically, Ezejideaku (2003) states that lgbo proverbs represent the world view of the lgbo society. Yusuf and Mathangware (2003) are of the view that proverbs are stratagems for dealing with situations. Petrova (2003) recognizes that proverbs can be used to control and shape a people's view of life. Brann (1977b) sees proverbs as being relevant for education policy planning and conflict resolution. Adeiyongo (2004) reveals that proverbs are effective medium through which teaching and moral instructions are carried out. Ashipu (2006) recognizes that proverbs function as a medium through which unlettered Africans expresses his experience about life. These findings of these scholars and others not captured here, as well as the present work, constitute an expanded definition and function of lgbo proverbs. This is because though some of them refer more specifically to other language groups and societies, but are aptly applicable to the definition and functions of lgbo proverbs. Additionally, the work shows that lgbo proverbs reveal the existence of linguistic and social inequality in the lgbo society as shown below.

Evidence of Linguistic Inequality in lgbo Proverbs

It is not always easy to uncover the sociological or sociolinguistic structures that abound in a given society. Only rigorous and extensive research helps to reveal such structural dichotomies that exist in both exotic and urban societies. For example, the discovery that differences between social classes are as clearly reflected in America as they are in Britain though the United States has the image of being much less class conscious, Hudson (2001). A Careful analysis of some proverbs in Igbo tends to reveal an identification and conferment of some measure of linguistic inequality on the users of Igbo language. Consider the following examples of such proverbs.

Igbo proverb: Onye a tuuru ilu kowaara ya, ego eji luo nne ya furu ohia.

Gloss: If a proverb is said to an Igbo native speaker and he did not understand it (expects an explanation), the money (bride price) used to marry the mother is considered a waste or useless.

Comment: The proverb above recognizes and makes a distinction in the Igbo society between

(a) 'Onye a tuuru ilu ya ghota ya' and

(b) Onye a turu ilu o ghotaghi ya.

(a) Refers to a group of those who do understand proverbs when it is said to them.

(b) Refers to the group of those who do not understand proverb when it is said to them.

By this proverb, the society is categorized into two major distinctive linguistic groups. It also gives a clue to the rating of the two linguistic groups. The linguistic group that understands the proverb when it is said to them, are adjudged to be more competent, fluent and possessing a mastery in the use of the language. The group that does not understand proverbs when it is said to them is adjudged to be incompetent, with little or no mastery in the use of the language. To say that, 'ego eji luo nne ya furu ohia' is to say that the person should not exist at all because if "the mother should not have been married," it means that the person should not have been born. It is a serious castigation and denigration of the linguistic status of those that cannot understand or make use of proverbs. This position projects a latent rule that associates competence and mastery of Igbo language to be significantly influenced by one's ability to use and interpret Igbo proverbs. The implication of this is that people in the family, community or society who effectively use proverbs in oral or literal expressions to teach, counsel, admonish and encourage etc are given a more prestigious linguistic status. Such appellations as, 'intelligent," "spokesperson", "wise person", "mouthpiece" or 'orator' etc is attached to them. Though suchopinion or judgment that informed this may be flawed or incorrect, but it has come to stay; subjective linguistic inequality.

Hudson's subjective linguistic inequality is concerned with what people think about each other's speech. In some societies like the Igbo society, some people are endowed with different levels of intelligence, friendliness and other such virtues according to the way they speak. Such judgment based entirely on speech may be quite wrong. Consequently, whatever virtues that are highly esteemed, some speakers are thought to have more of them than they really have, simply because they have the right way of speaking and others thought to have less because their speech conveys a wrong impression.

On the basis of Hudson's second linguistic inequality theory: strictly linguistic inequality, the Igbo proverb we are using, still portrays its manifestation. "Those who do not need any explanation to decode any Igbo proverb" are regarded as possessing some sort of compact vocabulary items that enable them not only able to decode any proverb but also to use any fitting proverb for any situation. They are assumed to possess a special array of rich proverbial terminology uncommon and unfamiliar with others. For example, in some sensitive or special events such as negotiation for traditional marriage rites especially; bride price, burial rites or naming ceremonies where their terminological skill is expedient, their presence or absence could make or mar the event.

In terms of communicative inequality, there tend to be an overlap between it and the strictly linguistic inequality as well as subjective inequality. If one knows enough proverbial terms but cannot use them appropriately either in understanding or in speech or other functional roles, he will be categorized among those "the money used to marry their mother is a waste" (ego e ji luo nne ha furu ohia) i.e. lower linguistic rating. Those who know and possess these special proverbial terminology items and apply them in communicative interactions are given high linguistic rating. They use it do decode an almost infinite number of proverbs in the language and also produce an almost infinite number of requisite proverbs in any given situation. This communicative competence based on their knowledge and use of the proverb recommends them to be chosen as masters of ceremony as well as umpires in coronation, wresting contest, birth and invocation events etc. Linguistically, they are considered superior to the others and subsequently we shall see how this translates to social inequality. This Igbo proverb evidently captures all three types of Hudson's linguistic inequality. Another proverb is given and analyzed below.

Igbo proverb: Nwata kwochaa Aka ya nke oma ya na ndi okenye erikota nri

Gloss: If a child washes his hands very well, he will eat together with the elders.

Comment: This proverb again distinguishes between two groups that exist in   the Igbo society namely, (a) the okenye (elders) and (b)nwata (children).

The okenye (elders) used in the proverb is not restrictive and strictly speaking of only elders or old people by age, father, it is a symbolic representation of a distinct linguistic and social group or class. This is also free of the use of the term nwata (children) in the proverb. The child (nwata) as used is not restrictive strictly in terms of age. It refers symbolically to a lower linguistic and social clans or group when compared with the other. Once again, this proverb recognises the existence of inequality in the Igbo society. The lower stratum represented by the term nwata (child) and the upper or higher stratum represented by the term ndi okenye (elders). The proverb further reveals that membership of any of the identified group is only not permanent but also flexible. There is linguistic or social mobility. This implies that one who belongs to the lower linguistic or social group can move up to the higher or upper class or group but not without satisfying certain conditions represented by, "Ikwocha aka ya nke oma (washing the hand very well). There could also be a movement from the upper class to the lower class which is not most desirable by many. As a matter of fact, the emphasis of the proverbs is on the need for hard work and diligence among the people, which characteristic can move somebody up from the lower class of society to the upper echelon. Linguistic competence (in the sense of our usage in this work) is one of the sustained efforts that could translate somebody from the lower to the upper class. The linguistic competence manifests in the use of the language which is significantly enhanced by the use of proverbs. An important yardstick in measuring the use of language in Igbo is the apt use and application of proverbs. A young person who grows up showing versatility and indepth in the knowledge and use of proverbs can easily be elevated to the council of elders or made to speak on behalf of the elders or to speak where the elders speak. He will be eulogized for possessing uncommon wisdom and intelligence. The effort to know, learn and use the proverbs is adjudged to be a process of "Ikwo aka nke oma (washing the hands well) which qualifies him to speak among the elders i.e. promoted to an upper class. Let us consider another Igbo proverb below.

Igbo Prov:	Otu nne na-amu mana obughi otu chi na – eke
Gloss:	One mother can beget many children but all the children will have different destinies.
Comment:	This proverb further demonstrates the existence of inequality in the Igbo society. It draws an extreme kind of analogy to reflect the deep noted linguistic and social inequality in the society by positing that even people born of the same mother (parents) may end up becoming unequal in language use and in social standing. It thus appears to be an affirmation of the already known truism in sociolinguistics that 'no two persons speak alike' even if they are identical twins because of individual idiosyncrasies that may be occasioned by pitch or

voice quality etc. The significance of this is that two people may be twins or of the same parents in Igbo society, may grow up having different levels of competence and ability in the use or understanding of Igbo proverbs. One may be grounded in the use and understanding of proverbs while the other can hardly decode or use a proverbs. As already noted in this work, this will place them in an unequal linguistic standing which will ultimately become also unequal social standing.

The Influence of Proverbs on Literary Assessment in Igbo

The use of Igbo proverbs significantly influences the assessment of written compositions in Igbo as well as any literary piece. Expression or language use (Asusu nka) is one of the criteria used to assess any written composition in Igbo language as it is also for English language at all levels of the school curriculum. Appropriateness of language used in writing the composition is one of the determiners of a good composition. This takes a significant part of the marks allocated for the composition among the positive qualities to be looked for under expression (Asusu Nka) include, clarity and appropriateness of style, for example range and aptness of vocabulary and collocation and judicious use of figurative language etc. In the judicious use of language appropriate use of proverbs and other figurative devices are prominently considered. A good application and use of proverbs gives a comparative advantage to any student's composition than that of another without appropriate use of proverbs as far as judicious use of figurative language and expression is generally concerned. On the overall, this could impact significantly on the passing or failing of the subject.

Furthermore, in the assessment of a good literary piece in Igbo, one of the criteria is the use of language which also includes the use of proverbs. A number of notable authors whose works are in Igbo language have endeared themselves to the heart of their readers with their mastery in the use of poetry. Such works include, Nwaozuzu's, Ajo Obi, (Drama), Ofomata's "Ugoma", Achara's "Elelia na Ile o mere Nzako's "Aka ji Ako" (prose) ,Chukwuezi's "Ako by Ndu", Madueke's "Nka Okwa," Ofomata's "Echiche m" (poetry). These are purely works written in Igbo language. Even such literary works written English language by Igbo scholars and writers such as Achebe's Things Fall Apart, No Longer At Ease etc have a reasonable number of Igbo proverbs.

The only difference in that in the books written in English language, the proverbs are translated into English Language. To assess a number of such literary works written in Igbo, especially in terms of language use, the apt use of proverbs will definitely influence the evaluation. Those with appropriate and sufficient proverbs will definitely stand out better adjudged in terms of appropriateness of style, judicious use of figurative language or expression is genera. Those that made no use of proverbs or made inappropriate use of them will be rated lower on the same aspects. This will to a large extent affect the overall assessment of the text. One can tend to say then that a significant influence of proverbs on literary assessment in Igbo leads to a kid of literary inequality where one text is considered superior to the other especially in terms of language use.

Linguistic and Literary Inequality as Social Inequality

Most of what we have done so far in work is to establish how proverbs give insight to and contribute to the existence of linguistic and even literary inequality in Igbo. This sub-section tends to demonstrate that the observed linguistic and literary inequality translates to social inequality. According to Hudson (2001:215) "Language, in the form of variety differences, contributes to social inequality by being used as a yard-stick for evaluating people..." The use of proverbs serves as yard-sticks for evaluating people and even literary texts. The three types of linguistic inequality posited by Hudson which through proverbs is seen to exist in Igbo society as demonstrated already, reveal an evaluation of people which lead to social inequalities. Those with high linguistic status tend to enjoy high social status while those with low linguistic status tend to be given low social status. Literary texts that are given high linguistic status tend to enjoy high social status and vice- versa. As observed in the work, on the basic of Hudson's subjective linguistic inequality, we discovered that when somebody has the ability to use and interpret Igbo proverbs in oral and written expressions and in various situations, the people evaluate him as of a high linguistic status. This high linguistic status translates to high social states. He is made to occupy certain socially, privileged positions in the family, village, town or society. Because they are seen to be "wise," "intelligent", "tough" or "learned," "orators", they are placed in a higher social, leadership or societal echelon. They are appointed members of the elder's council, masters of ceremony, spokesman of the people, conflict resolution experts, umpires in traditional rites such as wresting contests, coronation, birth and naming ceremonies, marriages, invocation /rituals, title / oath taking etc. It is interesting to note that those who can seldom express themselves in the mother tongue nor who need to be interpreted any proverb given in the language can hardly fill- up such positions. To understand the level of linguistic and social inequality promoted by the use of proverbs in the Igbo society may not be easy to an outsider without a comparative reference to what happens in the large and possibly more formal settings.

In a FIFA recognized football match for example, no person can be appointed a linesman, let alone a centre referee without being FIFA barged. To be a FIFA badged referee, one must have possessed appropriate professional skills, trainings and qualifications. In the Igbo linguistic communities, the appointment or elevation of one into such linguistic and social positions like being an umpire in a tradition wrestling match, being a family spokesman in a two family negotiation of bride price and marriage rites etc tend not to be based on academic qualification or professional training, but more on linguistic competence which manifests more in their apt use of proverbs. Their knowledge and ability to select appropriate linguistic items in relevant situations and occasions tend to make them socially unequal with others without such ability. The linguistic and social inequalities are further triggered by the ability to use the known and selected linguistic items for effective communication and interaction.

The attempt to know and use proverbs is accepted as one of the social refining processes that one need to undergo to move upwards from a lower social class to an upper social class. People's perception and evaluation of a man or child tend to improve as his knowledge, understanding and appropriate use of proverbs improves in the Igbo society. On the other hand, the perception and evaluation of a man or child tend to decrease as his knowledge, understanding and appropriate use of proverbs decrease. The Igbo proverb gives us an insight into the flexibility of this status movement in the Igbo society. We further understand that linguistic inequality more than biological or genetic relationship enhances social inequality in the Igbo society (Otu nne na- amu mana obughi otu chi na-eke). Certain traditional secret societies like the Okonko, place premium on the ability to speak and understand proverbs as one of the significant criteria for admitting members to the group. The social status and role of such societies in the Igbo society cannot be underestimated.

The use of proverbs influences the linguistic status which also influences the social status of a text or another. When an author makes good use of proverbs, he is said to be a "good author" and his text tend to be regarded very highly. The book is recommended or selected for wider use and the author could be recommended and selected for an award in preference for a book or author that did not make good use of proverbs. The literary inequality occasioned by the use of proverbs thus, leads to social inequality.

Conclusion

In addition to what has been said and written about proverbs, in this work, we have seen additional role of proverbs where it reveals and promote linguistic inequality which translates to social inequality. In the Igbo society in particular, knowledge and use of proverbs, tend to be considered more than academic and professional qualifications in the appointment, selection or elevation into prestigious and sensitive positions in the highly traditional settings. In fact, in some cases, the admittance of membership into certain cultural societies tend to be restricted to among other things, those with adequate knowledge and use of proverbs. We therefore conclude that proverbs not only give evidence of linguistic and social inequality in Igbo, but significantly determine the social and literary status to which one belongs. It is not just the palm oil with which they eat words.

References

Achara, D (1964). *Elelia na Ihe O Mere*. Ibadan: Longman

Achebe, C. (1958). *Things Fall Apart*. London: Heinemann

Adeiyongo, J. (2004). Language and Education: Proverbs as a Means of Instruction in Traditional Tiv Society. *International Journal of Linguistics and Communication*, Maiden Edition, 253-262

Ashipu, K. (2006). The Values and Functions of Proverbs in African Traditional Discourse. In O. Ndimele, C. Ikekeonwu and B. Mba (Eds.) *Language & Economic Reforms in Nigeria,* (PP. 125-135). Port-Harcourt: M & J Grand Orbit.

Bhuvaneswar. C. (2004). "Metaphoricity in Proverbs: A Karmik Lingusitic Analysis". National Seminar on Theortical and Applied aspects of lexical Semantics. Hyderabad: Osmania University

Brann, C. (1977). The Role of Language in Nigeria's Educational Policy: Some Comments and Inferences. Nigerian language teacher, 2,33-38.

Chukuezi, A. (1988). *Ako Bu Ndu.* Ibadan: Longman

Ezejideaku, E. (2003). Disability and Disabled. *Proverbium* 20 (2003) Vermont University, Vermont: Vermont, 159-170

Finnegan, R. (1970). *Oral Literature in Africa.* Oxford Clarendon Press

Hudson, R. (2001). *Sociolinguistics,* Cambridge: Cambridge University Press.

Iloene, G. (2007). Igbo Phonology. In O. Yusuf (Ed.) *Basic Linguistics for Nigerian languages Teachers.* (PP.163-194). Port Harcourt: Lan and Grand Orbit.

Madukwe, J (1979). *Nka Okwu.* Ibadan: Longman.

Mele, M. (2006). Nigerian Languages and Conflict Resolution: The Case for Proverbs and figurative Expressions. Paper presented at the 20th Annual Conference of the Linguistic Association of Nigeria. University of Abuja, Nigeria.

Nwaozuzu, G. (1998). *Ajo Obi* Enugu: format.

Nzeako, T (N.D). *Aka ji Aku,* Ibadan: Longman

Ofomata, C (1999). *Echiche M.* Enugu: Format

Ofomata, C (2001). *Ugonna* Enugu: Format

Petrova, R. (2003). Comparing Proverbs as Cultural Texts.20 (2003): Vermont university, Vermont: 331-3,4

Ridout, R and Willing C. (1967). *English Proverbs Explained.* London. Pan Books

Journal of Integrative Humanism – Ghana: Vol. 4 No. 1, October, 2014, ISSN: 2026-6286

ANAXIMANDER'S CONCEPTION OF THE URSTOFF AND THE IDEA OF NKE-MBU IN INTEGRATIVE HUMANISM

BY

OGBONNAYA, LUCKY UCHENNA
ESSIEN UKPABIO PRESBYTERIAN THEOLOGICAL COLLEGE
ITU
revluckyuogb@gmail.com

ABSTRACT

The crux of this work is that philosophies are inter-related. This can be found in the philosophies of Anaximander and the integrativists. It therefore asserts that although Anaximander and the integrativists lived in different philosophical epochs and geographical areas, they put forward a concept of the *urstoff* that is closely related. The relationship lies in their positing that the *urstoff* is something that is abstract, infinite, eternal and immutable. This is the point of their convergence. The point of their divergence is that, while the integrativists hold that the *urstoff* is known and it is Nke-Mbu – God, Anaximander holds that it is indeterminate and unknown. This conclusion is reached through critical analysis and synthesis of text.

Key-Words: *Apeiron, Integrative Humanism, Nke-Mbu (Nke-Mbu na Mbu), Urstoff, Uwa Mgbe Ebeiebi, Uwa Mgbe Nta.*

Introduction

This work seeks to bring out the relationship that exists between Anaximander's philosophy and integrative humanism. This relationship is found in their concept of the *urstoff* of the cosmos and realities. These two philosophies in discussing the *urstoff* are after answering questions about the one and many, unity and diversity (plurality), and change and changeless (permanence).

Background to the Philosophy of Anaximander

Anaximaner was a pre-Socratic philosopher who lived in Miletus, a city of Ionia (in modern day Turkey). He belonged to the Milesian school and learned the teachings of his master Thales. He succeeded Thales and became the second master of that school where he counted Anaximenes and arguably, Pythagoras amongst his pupils. According to available historical documents, he is the first philosopher known to have written down his studies, although only a fragment of his work remains (en.wikipedia.org/wiki/Anaximander). This is to

142

say that "Anaximander was the author of the first surviving lines of Western philosophy" (www.iep.utm.edu/anaximan/).

Anaximander's contribution and thought to knowledge has a wider range, as his thought touches several field of knowledge. His thought covers both philosophy (speculative philosophy) and science (natural philosophy). This connotes that Anaximander did not only put forward philosophical ideas, but also scientific ideas. Anaximander is believed to have contributed to knowledge in the areas or fields of astronomy, biology and evolution, cartography and geography, mathematics and cosmology. This could be the reason why a web material notes that

> He was an early proponent of science and tried to observe and explain different aspects of the universe, with a particular interest in its origins, claiming that nature is ruled by laws, just like human societies, and anything that disturbs the balance of nature does not last long. (en.wikipedia.org/wiki/Anaximander)

It is premised on his wide range of knowledge that cuts across several fields that he gave to the world of philosophy and science what cannot be forgotten. This man is indeed a great scholar that has affected the world of philosophy and science in no small measure.

On his contribution to astronomy, a web material posits that

> Anaximander was the first astronomer to consider the sun as a huge mass (and therefore to realize how far from the Earth it might be), and the first to present a system where the celestial bodies turned at different distances. He built a celestial sphere, and his work on astronomy shows that he must have observed the inclination of the celestial sphere in relation to the plane of the Earth to explain the seasons. Anaximander also speculated on the plurality of worlds, which places him close to the Atomists and the Epicureans who, more than a century later, also claimed that infinity of worlds appeared and disappeared. (en.wikipedia.org/wiki/Anaximander)

This could be the reason why "Anaximander is sometimes called... the founder of astronomy" (www.philosophybasics.com/philosophe...) since he discussed a lot of astronomical issues and observations.

In the field of biology and evolution, some consider Anaximander to be the earliest proponent of evolution (even though he had no theory of natural selection). Noting the existence of fossils, he claimed that animals sprang out of the sea long ago, and he put forward the idea that humans had to spend part of this transition inside the mouth of big fish to protect themselves from the earth climate, until they had time to adapt to the emergence of dry land (en.wikipedia.org/wiki/Anaximander). It is also believed that Anaximander does not only see humans as staying in the mouth of fish, but posited that human beings evolved directly from fish. His reason is that fish has longer time of parenting than any other animal; and this is closer to the time of parenting of humans. With respect to cartography and geography, it has been argued by geographer Erastosthenes that both Strabo and Agathemerus (later Greek geographers) agree that Anaximander was the first to publish a map of the world (en.wikipedia.org/wiki/Anaximander). In other words, he is believed to be the first to draw a map of the world that acted as guide to both traders and travellers.

His other interests were in mathematics (he explained some basic notions of geometry and introduced the sundial gnomon to Greece), metereology (he attributed some phenomena, such as thunder and lightning, to the intervention of elements, rather than to divine causes, and he explained rain as a product of the humidity of pump up from Earth by sun) (en.wikipedia.org/wiki/Anaximander).

On his cosmological theory, Anaximander gave a mechanical model of explaining the world as he asserts "the Earth floats very still in the centre of the infinite, not supported by anything" (www.philosophybasics.com/philosophe...). This material goes on to assert that

> He envisioned the Earth as a cylinder with a height one-third of its diameter, the flat top forming the inhabited world, surrounded by a circular oceanic mass. This theory allowed for the concept that celestial bodies could pass under or around it. (www.philosophybasics.com/philosophe...).

Also in his cosmology, he asserts that everything originated from the apeiron (the 'infinite', 'unlimited' or 'indefinite') (www.britainica.com/../Anaximander). This is a metaphysical concept. It based on this that he is called the first metaphysician. It is this area of his thought that will be given due consideration in the next section.

The Urstoff in Anaximander's Philosophy

Anaximander is a philosopher who did his philosophizing within the ancient period. At this period, the main concern of the philosophers was the primary stuff of reality or the universe. That is to say, they "proposed... the early philosophical views of reality" (Velasquez 42). "They raised the question about the ultimate nature of things and made the first halting but direct inquiry into what nature really consists" (Stumpf 8). Each of the philosophers in this period put forward what they understood as the urstuff. This is to say that they gave various views on the principle behind all realities in the universe. For instance, Thales sees this primary stuff to water. Aristotle puts it thus:

> Thales... says the principle is water (for which reason he declared that the earth rests on water), getting the notion perhaps from seeing that the nutriment of all things is moist, and that heat itself is generated from the moist and kept alive by it (and that from which they come to be is a principle of all things). He got his notion from this fact, and from the fact that seeds of all things have moist nature, and that water is the origin of the nature of moist. (Bk. I: Ch.3)

"Anaximenes designated *air*s as the primary substance from which all things come" (Stumpf and Fieser 10). This is believed to be also the view of Diogenes. Xenophanes of Colophon is of the position that earth is the primary element of things. He also asserts that all things that come into being and grow are earth and water (Owens 24). To Heraclitus, fire is the primary stuff. Put differently, the principle of things is fire. As for Empedocles, there are four basic elements from which things are made. Ozumba captures the thought of Empedocles thus:

> He accepted the reality of the four basic elements of Water, Air, Earth and fire as presented by Thales, Anaximenes, Xenophanes, and Heraclitus. He says that these four elements do not change. Their combination and disintegration are responsible for change and multiplicity. All things are made up of particles of these basic, unchanging elements. This means that actually, nothing comes into being except through these basic roots. What we have is the mixing and separating off of the mixture. (64)

It is the harmonizing of these four elements (Water, Air, Earth and fire) that leads to the formation of all realities in the world as there are today. This makes Empedocles a synthetizer, who did not propound any new idea but rather welded together the ideas of his predecessors.

It was in the midst of these philosophers of the ancient period that Anaximander came into the picture of philosophy. He was also worried about the question of the one and many (unity and plurality), change and permanence as well as the primary stuff of the cosmos. But contrary to the views of other ancient philosophers he proposed the indeterminate or *apeiron* as the primary stuff of things which is unchanging and is the unity in all things. It is this thought that the next paragraphs will focus on.

Anaximander like other Greek Philosophers of his time was also concerned about the *urstoff* of the cosmos. He believed that the cosmos and everything in it did not exist without any primary source. This is the view that he holds alongside Thales and other "Presocratic thinkers who tried to explain the nature of substance (or things) in concrete terms" (Jacquette 67). But with respect to what this *urstoff* is, he disagrees with Thales and other Ionian philosophers of his time. They all see the primary stuff of reality as concrete things, whereas Anaximander sees it as an abstract thing. A web material captures his view thus:

> There cannot be a single, simple body which is infinite, either, as some hold, one distinct from the elements, which they then derive from it, nor without this qualification. For there are some who make this (i.e. a body distinct from the elements) the infinite, and not air or water, in order that the other things may not be destroyed by their infinity. They are in opposition one to another – air is cold, water is moist, and fire hot – and there are, if anyone of them were infinite, the rest would have ceased to be by this time. Accordingly they say that what is finite is something other than the elements, and from it the elements arise. (en.wikiquote.org/wiki/Anaxiamander)

Anaximander debunked Thales' view that water is the primary stuff of the universe due to the fact that water is a perceptible entity. In his opinion all perceptible elements or entities are definite, limited and undergoes change hence, they cannot subsist on their own. Based on this, a perceptible entity cannot be the primary cause of things. According to John Ofem Inyang,

> Anaximander came up with the view that before all perceptible bodies there must be something that is indefinite without any implication of incompatibility and different from the corporeal bodies which serves as the primary source of all things. (154)

And anyperceptible is matter and matter undergoes change, which destroys it. In the words of George James, "Anaximander must have supposed that change destroys matter" (37), hence water and other matter cannot be the primary stuff of reality. This is because change destroys them. In the view of Joseph Omoregbe

> The primary element of all things, according to him (Anaximander) cannot be any of the things we know because all the elements we know are in conflict with each other and if any of them were the original stuff it would simply conquer and submerge the others. (72)

By implication, if water was to be the primary source of things in the cosmos, all things could have turned into water because it would seek to manifest itself above other existing things which are its opposite. This is the principle of injustice since water will seek to invade and subdue all things that it constitute, and then exist alone. In line with this, Federick Copleston notes that

> He (Anaximander) sought like Thales, for the primary and ultimate element of all things, but he decided that it could not be any one particular kind of matter, such as water, since water or the moist was itself one of the "opposites", the conflicts and encroachment of which had to be explained. (24)

He also notes that:

> If change, birth and death, growth and decay, are due to conflict, to the encroachment of one element at the expense of another, then on - the supposition that everything is in reality water – it is hard to see why the other elements have not long ago been absorbed in water. (24)

What he is saying is that if water is the ultimate stuff of the earth all things could have been turned into water. This is as stated earlier the principle of injustice. It is because other existent realities or elements are nothing and cannot exist without water. Water is a determined element. And as a determined element, it is like other elements hence cannot be the ultimate source of other determinate elements. All he is saying is that determined stuff cannot be the primary source of other determined things. Godfrey Ozumba and Michael Uka summarize this point thus:

> It must be remembered that though Anaximander agreed with Thales that there is one real, basic stuff, that is in process, he differed with Thales both about what this stuff is and about the nature of the process by which it becomes the many.

> Anaximander's contention is, is that nothing particular can give rise to the sundry things in the universe. He was of the view that anything that has the capacity for producing all other things must also have the capacity of accommodating those other things. He says that since water is specific, that it cannot possibly be the reservoir of all the multitudinous things we have in the world. (13)

What Ozumba and Uka are saying is not restricted to water, but to all determined and known elements. They do not have the capacity to produce and accommodate other elements or realities.

It is premised on this disagreement with Thales that a determined stuff is the source of all things in the cosmos that "Anaximander ... maintained that the basic substance out of which everything comes must be even more elementary than water and every other substance of which we have knowledge" (Moore and Bruder 19). What we know, for Anaximander, cannot be the primary stuff of the earth or things in the universe. He is of the opinion that the primary stuff of things is 'apeiron.' Apeiron is a metaphysical substance that is not known. It is indefinite, indeterminate, infinite, limitless, invisible, intangible and unchanging. This substance or ultimate reality can subsists on its own. "It is both uncreated and indestructible" (Aristotle Bk II: Ch. 3). It is eternal and boundless. In the words of Inyang,

> Since this element is eternal and as such cannot perish, it becomes the origin of all things and author of their changes (divine) for that which enables others to change must be changeless. This eternal, infinite, ageless and boundless primal substance which encompasses all the worlds transforms into the various substances around us and into each other. (154)

All determined realities or things spring from this apeiron which "is not qualitatively determined" (Onyewuenyi 169). This is the underlying principle of everything that exists.

Thus, apeiron which is a substance that can neither be created nor destroyed is the first principle of existence and will be the last principle of existence. This is what is implied in the remark of Bertrand Russell which reads: "into that from which things take their rise they pass away once more, as is ordained; for they make reparation and satisfaction to one another for their injustice according to the appointed time" (130). By this, apeiron is the principle of justice in the cosmos. It does not give room for any determined element to dominate other elements. All realities or things in the universe are equilibrated by apeiron – the principle of justice. From this it can be said that apeiron is "the primordial mixture of all the opposites" (Inyang 155). Apeiron is not only eternal but is an eternal motion which causes or enables other various specific elements come into being as separating from the original substances (Stumpf 7). It is in this sense that James says it is "the mythological notion of chaos" (37). It is the cause of existence and motion in the world while itself remains uncaused and unmoved.

Integrative Humanism: An Overview

Integrative humanism which is also known as "Njikoka Amaka" philosophy is a philosophical system developed by Godfrey Ozumba, a professor of philosophy in the University of Calabar, Nigeria. This philosophy proposes a method of philosophy that transcends African boundary. It is both a philosophy and a method as he captures it, "Integrative humanism is both a philosophy and a method of doing philosophy" (Ozumba, *Philosophy and Method* 22).

> Integrative humanism as a philosophy adopts a guided but open attitude in approaching issues of knowledge as they affect humans directly or indirectly. This attitude takes a serious view that all parts of reality constituting matter and spirit, the plant and animal world as an integrated ecosystem of which no part can be isolated without dire consequences. Integrative humanism as a philosophy can therefore be applied as a beneficial approach in studying any facet of existent reality. (*Philosophy and Method* 23)

Also,

> Integrative humanism becomes a method when it is articulated and used in interpreting a mass of reality or an instrument in conducting a research or as a way of bringing a new understanding to bear on old facts. For instance, a student applying the method of integrative humanism in research may want to know what different positions exist, and what constitute the limitations of these different positions (of say half truths) and how an integrative approach of shifting and welding can bring about a better or more acceptable harmonious whole. (*Philosophy and Method* 23)

Thus, it is a philosophy and method that seeks to harmonize more than one method or philosophy in explaining reality. This, for the integrativists, is the theory of integration. Ozumba therefore explains his philosophy based three concepts which operate on the principle of integration. These three concepts are found in electronics, mathematics and Njikoka Amaka. Godfrey Ozumba and Jonathan Chimakonam buttress this thus: "this is derived from insights from electronics and mathematics and further still, from Igbo-African injunction Njikoka Amaka" (6). This appears to be a bit contrary to Ozumba's previous idea that integrative humanism is derived from mathematics, electronics and sociology. It is not a contradiction but rather an addition of another concept that has informed the development of integrative humanism. This new concept that is found in *Njikoka Amaka: Further Discussions on the Philosophy of Integrative Humanism* is 'Njikoka Amaka'. In this new work the sociological inspiration is not mentioned. It is germane to state here that instead of holding to three inspirations to integrative humanism it is held that there are four inspirations, which include: mathematics, electronics, sociology and Njikoka Amaka.

On the mathematical and electronics influence on integrative humanism, Ozumba writes that

> Integration is derived from its root mathematical word 'intergers' which means 'whole number'. Insight from electronics talks of integrated circuit or micro-circuit. This means the assembly of electronic components fabricated as a single unit. It has to do with the interconnections of capacitors and resistors on a substrate to form a unitary structure. These insights from mathematics and electronics have fired my conception of how this concept can be deployed towards profitable philosophical utilization. (*Philosophy and Method* 11)

Ozumba anchors his argument on the relevance of social science to integrative humanism on cultural integration. According to him, cultural integration thrives on the concept of coherence, wherein "the diverse parts of any culture normally cohere in some fashion. Cultural integration is an aid to explanation, an aid to description, an aid to innovation, as a force in social cohesion" (13). On the relevance of Njikoka Amaka, he notes with Chimakonam that "also from the Igbo culture, integrative humanism derives its ... inspiration from the injunction 'Njikoka Amaka' which translates to 'to integrate is better than to disintegrate'" (7). These four concepts help to bring out the idea of integrations of various concepts and theories that aid insightful knowledge of reality. This discussion is possible through its method.

The method of integrative humanism is known as 'integrativism'. This method of philosophy is synthetic, since it brings together more than one methods to approach or understand reality. Lucky Ogbonnaya explains this thus:

> It synthesizes existent methods or approaches as well as theories of studying reality. It is also open to future philosophical methods that may be postulated since philosophy seeks to explain reality, which is still unfolding itself. Hence, it does not see any philosophical method or system as superior, or more important than others. Instead of disregarding any method or theory, it integrates them based on their usefulness in order to arrive at a better understanding of reality. And when they are not useful they are not discarded, rather they are kept and used where and when they are needed. It does not see philosophical methods, systems or theories as complete in themselves or competing rivals but as what should be integrated to have a clearer picture of reality. (4)

This is to say that it involves more than one method. With this, it can be called "polymethodic approach to reality. In other words, it is a multi-dimensional method used in approaching reality" (Ogbonnaya 3). It is in this light that Ozumba asserts that:

> Every ladder and equipment that will aid us to climb out of ignorance or what Asouzu calls the "the phenomenon of concealment" and which the Holy Writ aptly captures when it says "my people are destroyed because of lack of knowledge" should be fully utilized. (*Integrative Humanism and Complementary Reflection* 154)

It is pertinent to note that even when he avers that integrativism involves the use of more than one method, it does not follow that all Paul Feyerabend's "everything goes" (348). It makes use of only relevant methods for the explanation of a particular reality while the irrelevant ones are drop. This does not imply that they are discarded. They are not discarded but are kept and used when and where they will be relevant as stated in the earlier assertion of Ogbonnaya. In attempt to give a better and more comprehensive understanding of reality, integrativism harnesses the strength of every existing methods or theories. Chimakonam, Asuo and Agu aver that:

> This method demands that a researcher understands the kernel of different methods, the weaknesses and strengths of these methods, so that he can weld together their strengths in studying a given reality. This implies that he must first of all seek to understand the subject matter of his study by finding out its physical and transcendental aspects, so that the approach will be broad based and not one-sided or rift with bias and narrow-mindedness. (54)

This helps to substantiate the view of Ozumba which reads thus:

> We have integrativism which is the method which seeks to penetrate our research with the potentials of exploring and harnessing the benefits of opposites, complementable units, theories and methods all with the view of vouchsafing a broader, more comprehensive understanding of reality. (*A Rejoinder* 26)

The main objective of integrative humanism is to achieve a "higher, deeper, more profound and more comprehensive picture of reality" (*Integrative Humanism and Complementary Reflection* 154). Hence, he discusses both the mundane and spiritual aspects of reality since for him reality is multi-dimensional. He tries to go beyond just explaining the physical dimension of reality as many philosophers have done, by proposing and discussing a spiritual dimension of it. It is based on this that he calls his philosophy "spiritocentric humanism or spirit-centricism" (Ozumba, *Philosophy and Method* 40; Edet 16). It is with this that Ozumba posits that human being is a reality whose existence transcends this world. This is to say that the human being is being unto eternity (Ozumba, "National Conscience..." 152). The human being is a being that moves from uwa mgbe nta to uwa mgbe ebi-ebi. In other words, the human being is translated from this temporal world to the eternal world, which is the dwelling place of Nke-Mbu. This is the metaphysical aspect (Nke-Mbu) of integrative humanism that the next section of this work will dwell on.

The Concept of Nke-Mbu in Integrative Humanism

Innocent Asouzu in his 'forward' to the book *Njikoka Amaka: Further Discussions on the Philosophy of Integrative Humanism* commenting on the notion of being according to the integrativists posits that

Besides, and true to their integrative commitment, they adopt a "Christian perspective" as the foundation of their "integrative ontology," and one they aver gives their theory "the most acceptance conception of being. Being is that which is, and the chief being is Nke-Mbu which in Christian parlance is called God", they claim. (i)

This is to say that the word for God according to the integrativist is Nke-Mbu, who is the first being in the order of beings, and as the first being it is the highest being. This Nke-Mbu is not only the highest of being that exists but is also a being that is eternal. It is a being that is neither created nor will be destroyed. It has neither beginning nor end. It is that which has being in existence and will continue to exist even when all cease to exist. Its existence is eternal. This being also exists in the eternal world which the integrativists call "uwa mgbe eb-ebi". According to Godfrey Ozumba and Jonathan Chimakonam, "The ultimate being is Nke-Mbu dwelling in uwa mgbe ebi-ebi i.e the eternal world" (25).

Thus, Nke-Mbu is a being that exists in uwa mgbe ebi-ebi and is believed to be the first being and the uncaused cause or the unmoved mover. It is that which brings other beings into existence. In the words of Ozumba and Chimakonam,

> And for a necessary being to exist, it must be the cause of another necessary or possible being and so on. This chain of causation cannot continue in infinity there has to be a necessary being whose existence is not caused which is the cause of all other necessary cum possible beings. It is this being that Christians call God. It is only God, then as self-caused being (causa sui) – (sui-generis means uncaused cause). Aristotle calls this ultimate being the unmoved mover but we Him Nke-Mbu-na-mbu. That is the only non-contingent being that is responsible for other possible being. (27)

All possible beings exist and move because of Nke-Mbu. It is through Nke-Mbu that they exist and have their being. They all cannot exist without Nke-Mbu. This is because they are all dependent beings while Nke-Mbu is an independent being that exist without an eternal or necessary cause. This is to say that

> There is need for a first cause, an unmoved moves, the uncaused cause of all things, the creator whose creation is

uncalled for and the genesis of all generations. This being is what is called in the Christian parlance God. To set God aside and to continue to seek for the "cause of the uncaused" is to wilfully seek to fathom the bottom of the bottomless pit. Indeed, the idea of God as the first cause sets the inquisitive heart of man at peace. It is better to have God the creator than to have an incomplete history of evolution. If for nothing else, the idea God is at once sensible. (Ozumba and Chimakonam 31)

Nke-mbu is the fusion point of all realities as well as the two worlds – uwa mgbe nta and uwa mgbe ebi-ebi. This is what Ozumba and Chimakonam meant by:

The interconnections holding the realities in both uwa mgbe ebi-ebi and uwa mgbe nta is what we call integrative ontology or Nke-mbu ontology because every being can be explained with reference to Nke-Mbu. Nke-Mbu may well designate God which is why integrativists say that it is not just Nke-Mbu but emphatically, Nke-Mbu-na-mbu meaning the One and The Only or The First and the Only. (26)

Nke-Mbu as the One and the Only or The First and The Only is the one through which all realities derive their being. Every reality has Nke-Mbu or spark of Nke-Mbu within them. This is what Ozumba and Chimakonam seek to establish as they comment on human being which is the crown of creation. They assert that "the bottom line is that man is a being with the spark of the divine or Nke-Mbu inside him" (76). Nke-Mbu is the primary stuff of all reality. This is to say that "Nke-Mbu represents unity as the first principle of nature" (Ozumba and Chimakonam 75). Thus, "all humans came from one stock, that is, from Nke-Mbu" (Ozumba and Chimakonam 75). Based on the fact that everything has Nke-Mbu and came from Nke-Mbu, they will also return to Nke-Mbu and be unified with it.

The journey of all earthly realities including man to get to uwa mgbe ebi-ebi is a quest to beat and overcome the influence of time. When this is achieved, one sees being in its true light, eternal, one and united in Nke-Mbu. (Ozumba and Chimakonam 23)

At this point "integers cease to exist on their own and are perfectly united to Nke-Mbu which means the First or the One" (Ozumba and Chimakonam 22). This is when all realities go into uwa mgbe ebi-ebi.

In the uwa mgbe ebi-ebi, every reality that was once an individual is in Nke-Mbu as part of Nke-Mbu as Nke-Mbu! On this score, the necessary link principle collapses because the web connectivity of realities has faded away. There are no realities anymore but reality; no differences but oneness, but no diversity but unity. (22)

Nke-Mbu as a unifying principle assimilates everything into itself just as it brought them into being from itself. That is to say, just as Nke-Mbu emitted everything from itself into existence it will absorb them at the end of uwa mgbe nta. Nke Mbu by this is the first being and the last being as well as the reality of realities.

Anaximander's Apeiron and Integrativists' Nke-Mbu: A Conceptual Comparison

Anaximander and the Integrativists posit ideas about the basic stuff of the universe and reality that are closely related. And it is these ideas that will be looked at with the view of pointing out their similarities as well as their differences. It is pertinent to start by stating their similarities. Anaximander and the Integrativists, from the above sections appear to be interested in the same concept. They are concerned with the primary cause of everything that exists or that is in existence. This primary cause can also be called the material cause of the cosmos and all existent realities. Both of them assert that the material cause of realities is an abstract entity. According to Anaximander, this cause which is known as *apeiron* cannot be material but transcendental. It is in this sense that Copleston notes that "it could not be any particular kind of matter" (24). In the view of the integrative humanists or integrativists, "the ultimate being is Nke-Mbu dwelling in uwa mgbe ebi-ebi i.e. that eternal world" (Ozumba and Chimakonam 25). This is to say that the material cause of reality, according to Anaximander and Ozumba, is not only abstract but metaphysical. It is also apparent in their belief that the primary stuff of reality is immaterial and cannot be identical or identified with any material thing. This is what Stumpf and Fieser say of Anaximander as they note that "Anaximander said this stuff is neither water nor any other specific element" (6).

Thus, what Anaxiamnder and Integrativists are saying is that the primary stuff of reality is not only an abstract or metaphysical entity but also not specific or describable. It is that which cannot be described within the human language and world. This could be the rationale behind what Stumpf says of Anaximander as he notes that "the primary substance out of which all these specific things come... is an *indefinite* or *boundless* realm" (6). This implies that Anaximander's *apeiron* is not found in this physical world but a metaphysical world – a world beyond this human physical universe. It is this world that Ozumba and Chimakonam called "uwa mgbe ebi-ebi" (23). This Ultimate Reality exists in this abstract, transcendental world that is the world of eternity. It is in this vein that Ozumba and Chimakonam translate uwa mgbe ebi-ebi as "the eternal world" (25). It is this same world that has been described by Anaximander as the "indefinite boundless realm" as started above.

It is necessary to note that the *urstoff* of the universe and realities is identical with its place of existence. Both Anaximander and Integrativists agree that the Ultimate Reality that is behind existence is eternal. As started above, the abode of this reality is eternal, indefinite and boundless. This implies that the abode of the ultimate reality has no limitation. In other words, this abode is not restricted to time frame like the physical world. It is a timeless place of existence. This is also the characteristics of the Ultimate Reality. Of this, Copleston notes the view of Anaximander thus: "it is το ἄπειρον, the substance without limits. Eternal and ageless..." (25). This is echoed by Stumpf and Fieser that "the original stuff is infinite or boundless" (6). This reality, according to the integrativists, is eternal and unchanging. It is here that it is quite distinct from other realities or things.

Anaximander and the integrativists are of the view that the originator of the cosmos and realities is itself the creator and uncreated. In the view of Anaximander, the *urstoff* is "the unoriginated and indestructible primary substance" (Stumpf and Fieser 7). In the view of the integrativists, it is the 'uncaused cause'. This is what Ozumba and Chimakonam meant by:

> And for a necessary being to exist, it must be the cause of another necessary or possible being and so on. This chain of causation cannot continue in infinity there has to be a necessary being whose is not caused which is the cause of all other necessary cum possible beings. It is this being that Christians call God. It is only God, then as self-caused being (causa sui) – (sui-generis means uncaused cause). Aristotle calls this ultimate being the unmoved mover but we Him Nke-Mbu-na-mbu. That is the only non-contingent being that is responsible for other possible being. (27)

This is to say that the Ultimate Reality is the cause and source of everything as well as the first existent reality. It is "the first principle of nature" (Ozumba and Chimakonam 75). In more simple words, everything has the *urstoff* (Nke-Mbu or *apeiron*) in it. It is found in everything. It "encompasses all the worlds" (Fragments 1-3, quoted in Copleston 25). Put differently, everything has Nke-Mbu or aspect of Nke-Mbu in them. This is what Ozumba and Chimakonam meant by stating that "the bottom line is that man is a being with the spark of the divine or Nke-Mbu inside him" (76). Nke-Mbu is the primary stuff of all reality. This is to say "Nke-Mbu represents unity as the first principle of nature" (Ozumba and Chimakonam 75). Thus, all realities is "from Nke-Mbu" (Ozumba and Chimakonam 75).

Furthermore, Anaximander and Ozumba do not only see the primary stuff of things as the uncaused cause or the First existent reality but also as the 'unmoved mover'. It has, according to Anaximander as noted by Stumpf, an eternal motion which originates in itself and not outside itself; but that it is this inert motion that causes motion in other things in the world as well as their coming into being. In the words of Stumpf,

> The indeterminate boundless is the unoriginated and indestructible primary substance of things, yet, he believes, it also has eternal motion. As a consequence of this motion, the various specific elements come into being as they "separate off" from the original substance. Thus, "there was an eternal motion in which the heavens came to be". First *warm* and *cold* were separated off, and from these two came *moist* and *air*. (9)

Not only did all things take their rise from this Ultimate Reality, but they will return to it according to Anaximander and Ozumba. This assertion is based on the fact that all realities have Nke-Mbu and came from Nke-Mbu, these realities will also return to Nke-Mbu and be unified with it since it is their source. Ozumba and Chimakonam buttress this thus:

> The journey of all earthly realities including man to get to uwa mgbe ebi-ebi is a quest to beat and overcome the influence of time. When this is achieved, one sees being in its true light, eternal, one and united in Nke-Mbu. (Ozumba and Chimakonam 23)

The above position is in line with what has been posited by Anaximander as stated thus: "into that from which things takes their rise they pass away once more, as is ordained; for they make reparation and satisfaction to one another for their injustice according to the appointed time" (Russel 130).

The point of divergence between Anaximander and the integrativists rests on what the primary stuff is. To Anaximander, the *urstoff* cannot be pinned down to any definite reality or thing. It is just an abstract entity that cannot be equated with any reality. But for the integrativists, the ultimate stuff of reality is Nke-Mbu. This Nke-Mbu, for them, is God – the Ultimate Reality. According to Ozumba and Chimakonam,

> It is this being that Christians call God. It is only God, then as self-caused being (causa sui) – (sui-generis means uncaused cause). Aristotle calls this ultimate being the unmoved mover but we Him Nke-Mbu-na-mbu. That is the only non-contingent being that is responsible for other possible being. (27)

God, by this, is the primary cause of everything that exists against Anaximander's position that it is indeterminate and unknown.

Although Anaximander and the integrativists posit that the primary stuff of reality rests on the metaphysical world, and ageless, eternal, infinite and immutable, they path way as Anaximander do not give any specific name for this eternal, infinite and immutable world. For the integrativists, this world where the Nke-Mbu resides is the uwa mgbe ebi-ebi. This world in the Christian parlance is heaven. It is necessary to note that Anaximander associates apeiron with chaos just as James posits of him that "the Apeiron is regarded as the equivalent to...the mythological notion of chaos" (37). This implies that the first cause of things is a disorderly reality. This is not the case with the integrativists Nke-Mbu. Nke-Mbu is an orderly being that created all things to be orderly. Disorder is far away from Nke-Mbu.

Conclusion

It is glaring from the foregoing that Anaximander and the integrativists propagate a philosophy, and in particular metaphysics that is closely related. Their relationship lies in the fact that they posit an idea of the cause of everything that resides not in the concrete world. For them, the ultimate stuff of the universe is a metaphysical entity and is found in the metaphysical world. They also aver that this entity is eternal, unchanging and infinite. But their point of departure is that for Anaximander, this primary stuff is indeterminate and unknown, while the integrativists hold that it is definite and knowable, and that it is God – Nke-Mbu or Nke-Mbu-na-mbu.

This Nke-Mbu or apeiron lives in the eternal world, but Anaximander does not give any definite name for this world. In the position of the integrativists, this world is the uwa mgbe ebi-ebi (heaven). These two philosophies have done well to give one, information on the primary source of everything that exists in the cosmos. By this, both philosophies give the cosmological origin of things and the cosmos. This is also known as cosmogony (theory of origin), as against the evolutionary theory of origin.

Works Cited

"Anaximander (Greek Philosophers)". *Encyclopedia Britainica.* www.britainica.com/../Anaximander. Web. Retrieved on 23.09.2014.

"Anaximander". Internet Encyclopedia of Philosophy. www.iep.utm.edu/anaximan/. Web. Retrieved on 23.09.2014

"Anaximander". *Wikipedia, The Free Encyclopeia.* en.wikipedia.org/wiki/Anaximander. Web. Retrieved on 23.09.2014.

"Anaximander". *Wikiquote.* (en.wikiquote.org/wiki/Anaxiamander). Web. Retrieved on 23.09.2014.

Aristotle. *Physica.* Trans. R. P. Hardie and R. K. Gaye. *Introduction to Aristotle.* Ed. Richard McKeon. New York: The Modern Library, 1947.

Copleston, Frederick. *A History of Philosophy. Vol. 1.* New York: Image Books, 1985.

Edet, Mesembe Ita. "Ozumba's Spiritocentric Humanism: A Conceptual Critique". *Journal of Integrative Humanism-Ghana. 3.1.* Accra: Emmpong, (May 2013). 3-18.

Fayerabend, Paul. *Against Method.* Ed. Furman and Avila. Caalifornia: Maryfield, 2000.

Inyang John Ofem. "Ancient Philosophy". *Logic, Philosophy & Introduction to Computer Science.* Ed. Princewill Alozie. Calabar: ELCROF, 2000. 150-201.

Jacquette, Dale. *Pathways in Philosophy: An Introductory Guide with Readings.* Oxford: Oxford University, 2004.

James, George. *Stolen Legacy,* New York: Philosophical Library, 1954.

Moore, Brooke Noel and Kenneth Bruder. *Philosophy: The Power of Ideas*, 6th Ed. new York: McGraw Hill, 2005.

Ogbonnaya, Lucky Uchenna. "A Critique of Ozumba's Spiritocentric Metaphysics".

Okeke, Jonathan, Oduora Asuo and Sunday Agu. "Philosophy and Method of Integrative Humanism: A Response". *Journal of Integrative Humanism-Ghana. 1.1.* Accra: Emmpong, (August 2011). 49-60.

Omoregbe, Joseph I. *Knowing Philosophy*. Lagos: Joja, 2008.

Onyewuenyi, Innocent C. *The African Origin of Greek Philosophy: An Exercise in Afrocentrism.* Enugu: Snaap, 1994.

Owens, Joseph. *A History of Ancient Western Philosophy.* New Jersey: Prentice Hall, 1959.

Ozumba, Godfrey Okechukwu and Jonathan Okeke Chimakonam. *Njikoka Amaka: Further Discussion on the Philosophy of Integrative Humanism (A Contribution to African and Intercultural Philosophies).* Calabar: 3rd Logic Option, 2014.

Ozumba, Godfrey and Michael Uka. *A Handbook of Ancient Western Philosophy.* Calabar: 3RD Logic Option, 2014.

Ozumba, Godfrey. "Ancient Peroid of Philosophy". *Logic and Philosophy.* Ed. Innocent Asouzu. Calabar: University of Calabar, 2002. 48-82.

Ozumba, Godfrey Okechukwu. "Integrative Humanism and Complementary Reflection: A Comparative Analysis". *Filosofia Theoretica: An African Journal of Invention and Ideas. 1.1.* Calabar: Jochrisam, (Dec. 2011). 151-170.

---. "Integrative Humanism: The Spirit of Contemporary Philosophy". *Journal of Integrative Humanism-Ghana. 2.1.* Accra: Emmpong, (May 2012). 52-63.

---. "National Consciousness, Value Reorientation and Identity: An Integrative Humanist Approach". *Journal of Integrative Humanism-Ghana. 3.2.* Accra: Emmpong, (March 2014). 147-155.

---. "Ozumba's Spiritocentric Humanism: A Critique-A Rejoinder". *Journal of Integrative Humanism-Ghana. 3.1.* Accra: Emmpong, (May 2013). 19-27.

---. *Philosophy and Method of Integrative Humanism.* Calabar: Jochrisam, 2010.

Russel, Bertrand. *History of Western Philosophy.* London: Unwin Paperback, 1979.

Stumpf, Samuel E. *Philosophy: History and Problem. 5ᵗʰ Ed.* New York: McGraw-Hill, 1976.

Stumpf, Samuel E and James Fieser. *Socrates to Sartre and Beyond: A History of Philosophy. 5ᵗʰ Ed.* New York: McGraw-Hill, 2003.

"The Basics of Philosophy". www.philosophybasics.com/philosophe...Web. Retrieved on 23.09.2014.

Valasquez, Manuel. *Philosophy: A Text with Readings.* Belmont: Walsworth/Thomas Learning, 2002.

Journal of Integrative Humanism – Ghana: Vol. 4 No. 1, October, 2014, ISSN: 2026-6286

RESPONSE TO CLIMATE CHANGE FOR SUSTAINABLE DEVELOPMENT: A HUMAN RESOURCE DEVELOPMENT APPROACH.

BY

*NWOSU, ANN FRANCIS & **NWOSU, FRANCIS MADUWUBA

*DEPARTMENT OF POLITICAL SCIENCE

**INSTITUTE OF OCEANOGRAPHY

UNIVERSITY OF CALABAR

ABSTRACT

Human resource management (HRM) holds the key for effective and efficient response to climate change impacts in Nigeria. The challenges of climate change impacts have called for intervening response. Its wide-spread effects in form of floods, droughts, desertification, rising sea level, changing rainfall patterns, rising temperatures and coastal storms among others have posed daunting problems to socio-economic and political systems thereby making it difficult for the attainment of sustainable development. Climate change is caused by man, now it has perverted virtually every sector of the economy such as Energy, Agriculture, Environment, Health, Industry, Transportation. Nigeria was one of the developing nations who were in the vanguard for promoting the global efforts geared towards the formulation of unanimous policies and strategies for combating the climate change impacts. She identified with the August 24, 1994 International Convention and December 10, 2004, Kyto protocol which took effect on March 2005 as well as 18th December, 2009 Compenhagen Denmark climate change summit in an effort to fight against climate Change impacts. However, the Institutional Framework such as NEMA, SEMA, NCCC established by the government lack adequate capability in terms of knowledge and technological expertise this has necessitated to implementation failure. HRM has been described as a panacea for labour incapacitation in the areas of adaptation, mitigation, emergency response and management. Governments are called upon to invest fund into research and development and private sector to partner with the government in sponsoring research and development. Inculcate science culture in all levels of education - primary, secondary tertiary and university in order to save and secure the future dispensation from the present dearth of labour and incapacitation in terms of sustainable development.

Key-words: *Climate Change, Sustainable Development, and Human Resource Development*

Introduction

Climate change has been described as a lasting change in the statistical distribution of weather patterns over periods ranging from decades to millions of years (Wikipedia). Again the UNFCC, 1994 referred to the climate change as a change of climate which is attributed directly or indirectly to human activity that alters the composition of the global atmosphere and which is in addition to natural climate variability observed over comparable time periods. Moreover, Barack Obama the US President described climate change as "the greatest challenge facing human kind. He made that description on the eve of the conference on climate change held in Copenhagen, Denmark in December 2009. There is a global concern about the climate change impacts in the globe as both developed and developing countries are affected by climate change impacts. However, its vulnerability is more prone to the developing countries.

The report of World Bank (2010) revealed that about 75 to 80% of the cost of damages caused by the climate change would be borne and are being borne by the developing countries. The impacts of climate change are directed to the economic, social and political system of the nations. The report of IPCC, (2007) highlighted that human element through the 'Green house effect' due to human - produced increased concentrations of greenhouse gases in the atmosphere and changes in land use resulting to Global warming or from Anthropogenic Global warming. The global means surface air temperature increased by 0.74 degreeCelsius and the global means sea surface temperature (SST) increased by 0.67 degree Celsius over the last century. Wikipedia, the free encyclopedia (1997) further explained that the common greenhouse gases easily known are those that manifest naturally which include water vapour, carbon dioxide, methane, nitrous oxide and ozone. The gases that came exclusively from human industrial process are hydrofluorocarbons (HFCs), perfluorocarbons (PFCs) and sulfur hexafluoride (SF^6). The World Bank (2010) study revealed that, 20°c warming above preindustrial temperatures which is the least the world is likely to experience could result in permanent reductions in GDP of 4 to 5% in Africa and South Asia. The simple interpretation being that these countries lack the capability in terms of finance, technology and expertise to manage the climate change impacts. Climate change impacts have gained international recognition as its devastation is raising global concern but the international action interms of response has been slow.

The first international response against climate change took place on

May, 9 1992 in New York, USA, under the auspices of the United Nations (UN) when the nations of the world gathered and calculated all the adverse effects of the nature of climate change and the dangerous nature of its predicted impacts. In order to protect the earth climate system from more anthropogenic effects and to produce or adopt strategy for response to ascertain its impacts the United Nations adopted Framework convention on climate change (UNFCCC). The convention was initiated on March, 1994 (Ibe, 2010). Again, an adjunct to the UN Framework Convention on climate known as 'the Kyoto Protocol' wasadopted on May 11 December, 1997 in Tokoyo, Japan by parties to the UNFCCC. Here binding targets were set for 37 industrialized countries known as Annex I countries and European community to reduce Greenhouse Gas (GHG) emissions. This strategy has provisions to assist countries especially underdeveloped countries to adapt to the adverse effects of climate change. One of such effects or impacts is global warming which is drawing attention of the entire world (Ibe, 2011). The December, 2009 Compenhagen, Denmark climate change summit according to the 'Baw Road Map', a framework for climate change mitigation beyond 2012 was to be agreed there. The goal was to cut greenhouse gas emissions by 30% in Europe, to cut carbon emissions by 15% in Keland on the 16th of December, 2009. The Guardian reported that the summit was in Jeopardy, "we have made no progress" said a source close to the talks. On 18th of December after a day of framtic negotiations, it was announced that a "meaningful agreement" had been reached, giving the world hope of positive and lasting response for change.

Nigeria following the international response to climate change impacts was most concern also in the area of adaptation to impacts of climate change variability, mitigation and emergency response and management. Adaptation here means to survive in the mist of climate change impacts. Mitigation is to reduce the climate change impacts, emergency response and management is rescue mission to the victims of climate change impacts. Nigerian combate so far against climate change is at low ebb but the nation is vulnerable to the impacts of climate change mostly because about 70% of Nigerians are engaged in small scale rain-fed agricultural production, the natural resource base is decreasing and the infrastructure base is decreasing and skewed in favour of those living in urban areas. (BNRCC, 2010). She lacks the capacity in terms of finance, technology and experienced experts to manage the climate change impacts. Just like her other African and South Asian countries, Nigeria is vulnerable to the climate change impacts in different areas specifically studies revealed that the large-marine Ecosystem will suffer from accelerated sea level rise, increased occurrence and intensity of storm surges with flooding and coastal erosion, progressive, salinization of fresh water aquifers resulting to short in supply of portable water, displacement of settlements, devastation of coastal vegetation, unpredictable variability unavailability of fisheries resources. People in coastal areas are prone to diseases example malaria. (Adegoke, 2010, Ibe, 2010, Ibe, 2011, Ibe and Ibe 2010). Thousands in coastal areas lose their lives, homes and property, crop failures, reduction in agricultural productivity (The World Bank, 2010). Climate change threatens to erode progress in economic growth and undermines prospects for sustainable development. According to Ibe and Ojo, (1994) climate change and associated sea level rise would have significant impacts on socio-economic activities in Nigeria. The sea-rise level will increase the vulnerability of coastal settlements. Ibe and Ojo, (1994) pointed that Port Harcourt, Warri, Lagos and Calabar located along the coast. In addition Lagos alone is reputed to have the population of 15 million. As the emergence of petroleum Industry has necessitated to large migrations to the coast. The incidence of flooding which took place in Nigeria in which about 21 states of Nigeria were affected portrayed and vividly explained what we mean by socio-economic dislocation. Federal Government spent N17.5 million for containment and sustaining families who were relocated to different temporary settlements. Global warming which is one of the impacts of climate change produces excessive heart leading to sun burn, heat rashes and other skin infections.

Climate change impacts cannot be controlled or managed naively without the utilization of appropriate management approach to quell its menace. Such approach as Human Resource Management approach, not minding the incessant pressures from interested pressure groups, the issue of climate change adaptation, mitigation, emergency response and management would continue to be a mirage and illusive unless human resource management approach is accorded a central position in Nigeria. Many ardent scholars in the field of political science and other social sciences have cautioned that Nigeria depending majorly on external assistance for technical experts, technology transfer and financial support would slow the progress in fighting against the challenges or threats of climate change impacts in Nigeria and other developing countries thereby making attainment of sustainable development impossible. Nigeria has enough workforce in terms of population but they need training and retraining and other inducement that is why HRM must be given a central place in Nigerian Public Administration.

Objectives of the study

(i) The major objective of this study is to determine various ways in which the utilization of Human Resources Management approaches can promote effective and efficient response to climate change impacts.

(ii) Ascertain the level of awareness of climate change impacts in rural communities.

Research Questions

(a) What roles does Human Resource Management play in creating awareness in the area of adaptation and mitigation of climate change impacts?

(b) In what ways does the quality of labour affect efficient and effective organization?

Statement of the problem

Nigeria was among one of the developing countries who were in the vanguard of promoting the global effort geared towards formulation of unanimous policies and strategies against the impacts of climate change. She was part and also in agreement with the August 24 1994 international convention and was in support of December 10, 2004 Kyoto protocol which came into force on March 15, 2005 despite all these much has not been done locally in terms of implementing the policies and showing adequate commitments in fighting against the climate change impacts.

No serious efforts has been made by Nigeria in terms of building strong institutional capability and effective labour force to enable her join the international struggle for the mitigation of greenhouse emission that induce global warming and creating awareness for adaptation to climate change impacts. The labour force in various institutional frameworks such as NEMA, SEMA and NCCC etc, lack adequate training and lack expertise in handling technology, utilizing human resource management approach perhaps is the panacea for responding to the institutional framework weakness or inability. The drafting of policies has not been a problem but proper implementation of policies has mostly been meeting with serious failures. This study therefore investigated various ways human resource management principles would promote effective efforts against climate change impacts in Nigeria.

The study is significant because it has revealed the capability of human resource management principles that may proffer solution to the identified climate change impacts in Nigeria and called the attention of the government to sensitize the communities on climate change impacts adaptation and mitigation.

Methodology

The study utilized both secondary and primary data collection. The secondary data was based on a desk review. The writers consulted existing literature on the subject which include; published works on climate change impacts and Human resource management.

The primary data was based on participant observation in the activities of some NGOs especially in the work of COLIN and CARUNDEP in which one of the writers fully participated under a field study which studied communities for analysis and assessment of awareness of climate change impacts adaptation and mitigation in rural communities. It was observed that rural communities are noticing changes in terms of sea level rise, low fish stock, lost of harvest but they did not understand that it was climate change impacts. They have no idea of the causes of their predicaments as climate change impacts, this means that they need to be educated about what to do and how to adopt and what not to do in order to mitigate the impacts.

Theoretical framework
Theory of Strategic Human Resource Management (SHRM)

According to Kelinger (1973) a theory is 'a set of interrelated constructs (concepts), definitions and propositions that present a systematic view of phenomena by specifying relations among variables, with the purpose of explaining and predicting the phenomena: Ndiyo (2005) pointed out that theories synthesize isolated bits of empirical data into a broader conceptual scheme of wider applicability and predictability. Alan Isaac explained that, the major function of a theory is 'explanation of empirical generalization; Mbipom, (2000) opined that 'a good theory is a guide to collection of facts'. Scholars in the field of social sciences agreed that 'a good theory is a guide to action'. Therefore, theory of Strategic Human Resource Management was selected to guide the actions of various institutional frameworks in utilizing HRM as it proffers various administrative principles in response to climate change impacts. Following Grace Mbipom's advice, 'a good theory provides guidance to an administrator when he wants to act.'

Strategic Human Resource Management (SHRM) is a new area which emerged in the last two decades. The major exponents are Hendry and

Pettigrew (1990). SHRM is focused on the relationship between human resource management and strategic organization. It concerns abroad areas relating to structure, culture, management and change, organizational effectiveness, performance competence, employee development and matching resources to future administrative requirement i.e. capable employees would be raised and utilized to achieve pre-determined organizational goals.

The major aim of SHRM is pointing to the capability of the management in handling the labour force in order to make them productive and efficient. To make the employees to activate their commitment, self motivation, dedication and focus to the organization. How to make employees to use their brains to make things work in terms of creativity, insight and imagination. Thus, SHRM proposes that the relationship between the management and employees should base on mutual respect, including shared form of decision-making. The management builds a strong, sense of collective responsibility for the success of the organization. This is done through the utilization of multi-sectoral approach, peer reviewed discipline, grounded conceptual and empirical research to areas of interests to the researchers, scholars and practitioners of strategic management and organization. It provides an international inter- disciplinary forum designed to improve understanding of the interrelated dynamics of strategic organization process and outcome.

SHRM is based on the assumption that there is a relationship between a range of possible external contingencies and human resource management (HRM) policy and practices. Strategies here means particular decision and actions adopted by the management in order to enable them accomplish performance objectives.

Institutional framework against climate change impacts

The Federal Government of Nigeria in her efforts to respond against the climate change impacts established under the Ministry of Environment a new Department for Climate Change. A centre for climate change and fresh water resources is set up at the Federal University of Technology Minna. The Department is created to implement the convention and the protocol activities. Its responsibilities is also to coordinate the activities of the inter-ministerial committee on climate change with representation from various ministries such as Finance, Agriculture, Water Resources, Energy, Commission etc.

Federal Government in realization that climate change adaptation and management, go hand in hand with poverty reduction integrated an agricultural policy in 2001 as an instrument to wage war against climate change impacts.

Objectives of Agricultural Policy are:

(1)   The achievement of self-sufficiency in basic food supply and attainment of food security.

(2)   Increased production of agricultural raw materials for industries.

(3)   Increased production and processing of exports crops using improved production and processing technology.

(4)   Protection of agricultural land resources from drought, desert encroachment soil erosion and food and general preservation of the environment for the sustainability of agricultural production.

(5)   Promotion of the increased application of modern technology to agricultural production and

(6)   Improvement in the quality of life of rural dwellers.

Strategy or the implementation of the agricultural policy - National Fadama project started in 1991. Its main objectives are to improve the quality of life of small holder farmers, food security and rural infrastructure.

In the aspect of emergency response and management, the Federal Government Established National Emergency Management Agency (NEMA) and State Emergency Management Agency (SEMA) by state governments under the vice president's office. NEMA was established by Act 12 and amended by Act 50 of 1999 constitution. The Federal Government trough the NEMA has the mandate to disaster management in Nigeria coordinate the activities of stakeholders in disaster management, coordinate plans and programmes for efficient and effective response to disasters in the country and promote research activities relating to disaster management in the country. Following the establishment of NEMA, the State Emergency management Agency (SEMA) was established in the states to meet with the challenges of increased rate of disasters and their attendant complexities. The SEMA serves as the primary coordinating agency for the operations plan. It carries out this role through its administrative and specialized activities. These activities include notification, planning, activation, mobilization, deployment, logistic support, communication and public information. The plan is inter-agency strategy. For managing disaster with emphasis on the principle of Incidence Common System (ICS) and the use of support service organizations such as communication, fire fighting, management, public works and engineering, mass care, Health services, search and rescue, Nutrition, Water and Sanitation, Security, Energy and Resource Support.

Upon identification of any impending or actual disaster, the local authority notifies SEMA, the Agency in turn issues an advisory notice to relevant agencies that may require action. SEMA's responsibilities include to plan, implement and coordinate all activities related to disaster management comprising - forecasting, prevention, preparation, response. Under response, you have search and rescue, evacuation, relief delivery and mass care. Other disaster management activities include: recovery, rehabilitation, resettlement, reduction, public education, establishment of early warming system and capacity building for stakeholders. The SEMA has the responsibility of collaborating and networking with other stakeholders such as NEMA, Red Cross, Civil Defence, Federal Road Safety Commission, the Police, and relevant government ministries, the Military, NGOs and the Communities for adequate response. Trado - Modern means of communication are often used to create awareness among the public on disaster issues (CR SEMA, 2012).

Central Bank of Nigeria (CBN) is among the institutions involved in response to climate change impacts. The CBN has established the Nigerian incentives - based risk sharing system for agricultural lending known as NIRSAL. It is a kind of insurance mechanism for the agricultural sector and incentive designed to stimulate innovations in agricultural lending by encouraging banks that are lending to the sector to eliminate state dependency by banks fordeploying loan-able funds to agriculture and ensure its sharing approach that will build business approach where banks share in the risk of lending to the sector. The loan beneficiaries are small scale farmers, medium to large scale farmers, agro business, agro-dealers and processors. Agriculture is the economic lifeline of Nigeria regardless of the significance of contribution of the oil sector to the Gross Domestic Product (GDP) of Nigeria. It pays more than 80% of rural dwellers, because it creates rural employment opportunities and has absorbs the significant size of the labour force. It helps to stem the tide of rural - urban migration. Given its significant role to the rural transformation, Nigerian regimes since 1976 have been putting serious efforts to revitalizing agricultural sector which has been partially neglected and marginalized as a result of oil industry (Arua and Duru, 2010).

Again, physical planning and building codes is part of the strategy being utilized for the response to the climate change impacts in Nigeria. These refer to the series of legal policy provisions that gave credence to physical planning activities. These include, land use Acts of 1978, Urban Development Policy of 1992, Urban and Regional Planning Act 1992 and the Housing and Urban Development Policy of 2002. Physical Planning Control measures have also been introduced to improve urban use planning and urban Development (National Capacity Assess Report 2012).

Moreover, the senate is also involved in the response against climate change impacts in Nigeria. The senate has a standing committee ecology (Senate Committee on Ecology) and the National House of Assembly has a standing Committee on Climate Change. The members are responsible for passing of Climate Change Commission (CCC) bill for both the House of Assembly and senate. There is also the National Council on the Environment (NCE) made up of representatives of governments at the Federal and state levels. The council meets at irregular intervals to take stock of the state of the environment in Nigeria. Part of this response to climate change impact is the formation of the House Committee on Climate Change (HCCC) which responsibility is to setup advocacy across the media, civil society, private sector, government and the proactive stands adopted by a number of states in Nigeria.

Despite all these institutional frameworks achievement on the areas relating to climate change impacts, adaptation, mitigations, emergency response and management has been low. Sustainable development is being threatened by a plethorea of climate change impacts such as flood, erosion, windstorm, landscape, desertification, loss of biodiversity, land degradation, deforestation, changing rainfall pattern, rising temperature, coastal storm are posing daunting threats on environment, animals and man. The institutional frameworks are fraught with limitations or obstacles which made them grossly in adequate and deeply limited. The institutional frameworks lack a comprehensive implementation strategy capable of translating the policies into concrete reality and into real inter-sectoral activities for sustainable environmental management and disaster risk reduction which could enable the polices become anticipatory adaptation and disaster prevention options for Nigeria. Plan implementation is one of the obstacles militating against development planning in Nigeria. Many good plans fail at the implementation stage. In his own view (Ibe, 2011) noted that the establishment of the institutional framework will overcome a common obstacle which is the lack of integration between economic and environmental decision making but it is clear that Nigeria will face certain challenges that have been identified in similar situations in other parts of the world. Some of these challenges were listed but not limited to the following: availability of funds, the paucity of technology, inadequate human resources skilled enough in handling modern technology, inability of evolving policies and creating or designing effective regulations and laws to enforce their implementation, plan indiscipline, corruption, and unclear goals. Lack of coordination, harmonization, and control and lack of adequate political will (Obande, 2007), politicization of the institution and indigenization limit the institutional framework. The department created from the Ministry of Environment to implement the convention and the protocol activities lacks the power to coordinate all the activities of the other inter-ministerial departments, academia and NGOs on climate change. It was not acquainted with the nature, content and level of adaptation, emergency management activities going on in the stakeholder ministries, academia and NGOs. On intellectual level, the frameworks represent bourgeoisie creation.

The grassroot were not involved. Wolfang Stolper taught that, success in adopting any plan would be achieved if both the grassroots and high level, policy makers are drawn into the formulation of the plan in the first place. This is known as 'bottom up approach, Unwadiegwu and Muoghalu (2012) reported that 'top down' approach failed in urban renewal policy in coal camp city Enugu State because the stakeholders and end users as in other cases resisted and revolted against the programme. Stolper emphasized that policy planners must have good personal relationship with the grassroots to understand how the people are feeling toward each policy that is why the people must be involved in the planning stage. DRRCA (2012) reported that irrespective of the existing physical planning robust laws and policies, urban centres in Nigeria are still plagued with problems arising from ineffective physical planning, ineffective and uncoordinated land use management in many states across the country. This trend has led to persistent problem of urban decay portrayed by increased slums and substandard housing condition and poor shelter condition in urban areas, overcrowding, poor sanitation, indiscriminate waste disposal, blockage of gutters leading to flood and poor quality houses.

Lastly, political scientists and other social scientists have noted and cautioned that Nigeria continuing depending majorly on external assistance of technical experts, technology transfer and financial support would slow the progress in fighting against the challenges or threats of climate change impacts in Nigeria including other developing countries. Those expatriate technical experts were trained and empowered in their countries, Nigeria should 'borrow a leaf' from them by engaging into training, empowerment and motivation of her workforce.

The issue of climate change adaptation mitigation, emergency response and management would continue to be a mirage and illusive unless Human Resource Management approach is accorded a central position in

Nigerian administration.

What is Human Resource (HRM) approach?

Human Resource Management approach has been defined as a distinctive approach to employment management which seek to achieve competitive advantage through the strategic deployment of a highly committed and capable workforce, using an integrated array of cultural, structural and personnel techniques (story, 2000), HRM is a strategic and comprehensive approach to managing people and work place, culture and environment. A scholar pointed out that organization's culture and style of leadership are the key to the understanding of what makes organization function. Culture plays a vital role in human resource management. Continuous utilization of expatriates who are unfamiliar with the culture and the environment of Nigeria's public sector may not yield the expected result in the issue of fight against climate change.

HRM is also defined as strategic approach to the management of humans resources that involve all management decisions and actions that affect the relationship between the organization and employees (Beer et al., 1984). Effective utilization of HRM enables the employees to contribute optimally to the overall organization success. HRM is expected to add value through the strategic utilization of the employees and that employees programmes impact on the organization in a measurable way. The point being made here is that in every organization whether private or public, it is not the equipment that work but the human element in the organization that are critical factor for the achievement of organizational goals/objectives. So attention is directed to human beings in the organization in order to build their capacity or capability. Oba (2005) says that managing the human component is the central and most important task because all else depends on it and how well this is done.

In the perspective of a nation, human resource underscore a concerted effort to improve the talents, skills, capability and endowments of the people and how these attributes are used to actualize the developmental aspirations of the society determines the levels of attainment of that nation in the development ladder. In other word, if a nation fails to develop her human resource or labour that nation would continue to suffer under development. The real capital of a nation or organization is the human capital. Quality training in form of education and technocraft enables an employee to perform. The possibility of this starts from the management. The management plans the work to be done, staff operations, organizes the work or task and directs the work and control the result by measuring performance against plan. Thus, commitment to the achievement of the objectives of policies of response to climate change impacts in terms of adaptation, mitigation, emergency response and management depends on effective performance on the part of the workers of NEMA, SEMA, the Ministry of Environment and all other inter-ministerial departments, academia, NGOs and even the people in the rural communities who are more prone to the climate change vulnerability. But such performance will depend to a great extent on their knowledge and skill and interest on the task committed into their hands to do.

Aso (2005) opined that despite the overwhelming salience of Human Resource Management, successive regimes in Nigeria both Military and civilian have neglected this important aspect of development and progress. The neglect of HRM has led to failure in the side of government to sponsor research and development in Nigeria and the failure to implement science and technology policy that will promote industrialization for sustainable development. So the country is still in low technological base. Most scientists are lacking in multidisciplinary research but depend on single purpose research. Obande, (2007) says that the problem is because the science and technology institutions are weak. The management begin the process of planning the goals of the organization but Drucker, (1999) observed that only few management have clear idea of their organizational goals and he believed this to be their worst mistakes.

The need for the Inclusion of HRM approach in the response to Climate Change Impacts

The need for the inclusion of HRM approach in the activities of governments in the response to climate change impacts arises because the HRM approach would bring into bear certain administrative principles that would enhance the activities and the effectiveness of NEMA, SEMA and other governmental agencies that are responsible for tackling the problem of climate change impacts. Principles like effective planning; organizing, coordination, directing and control would create room for efficiency, economy and equity. Giving the nature of the duties of the institutional framework they need to plan for contingences. These administrative principles by HRM in the battle against climate change impacts specifically will play the role of manpower planning for the purpose of recruitment selection, socialization, appraisal, training development and motivation of labour who in the long run will be equipped with experience, skill and talent and will be able to execute planned programmes and projects for the curtailment of climate change impacts. This will improve the living standard of the populace.

HRM would utilize the principle of financial administration as a tool against the challenge of climate change through the budgeting process, control of public expenditure, accounting and auditing. With the awareness that no government programme can advance without proper funding, therefore this principle would enable the government to realize that the success of NEMA, SEMA and others' projects can only progress depending on the volume of money pump into them and judicious spending of the money Anam (2012). It is government culture to hold their administrators accountable, thus NEMA, SEMA etc would be held accountable to the way they used and spent the funds committed into their hands in all their operations. This would only be made possible through the principle of administrative, accountability which makes it possible for all misuse or abuse of powers and corrupt practices to be accounted for. This will be achieved if HRM is given its proper place in the government administration.

Again, HRM will bring In the principle of citizen's chapter which empowers the citizens as target group to demand from NEMA, SEMA etc basic accountability, transparency, probity, quality and choice of service. When the people make distress call they would be attended to without delay.

HRM would also bring in the principle of public and private partnership. Government partnering with private sector and NGOs will enhance the efforts against climate change impacts. It will enable the government to raise trillions of naira for adaptation and mitigation solution.

HRM through comparative administration would ascertain thedifferences and similarities on the problems of climate change impacts in Nigeria and other African countries. Comparative administration used by HRM would make the evaluation of the damages caused by climate change impacts possible. The comparative administration will focus on cross national and cross cultural comparison in different countries to bring out the knowledge of impacts of climate change disruption in diverse countries. The experiences of people who are most vulnerable to climate change would also be noted, impacts of the institutional framework created to fight against climate change issues and other disasters would also be evaluated, the behavior and awareness of people to climate change impacts would be evaluated. Through the comparative administrative principle, the professional or experts in the field of Metrology may be able to predict the events and trends that trigger the climate change and would be able to sensitize or educate people towards proper attitudinal behaviours. HRM would apply the development Administration as an administrative instrument in the struggle against climate change impacts. As an innovative tool, the management of the government institutions and agencies i.e. NEMA, SEMA etc assigned with the duties of responding to climate change impacts would acquire new skills and new ideas with new vision, insight, creativity and imagination that will enable them In rendering community services, programme planning and implementation project management and development that would improve the living standard of distress families in terms of giving reliefs, evacuation and building concentration camps, giving necessary drugs to those who are sick, teaching people to maintain proper sanitation in order to avoid outbreak of epidemics and so on. Also building or creating alternatives to their former source of livelihood in terms of adaptation. The institutional frameworks have a lot to gain by using HRM approach as fecundous tool in their response to climate change impacts.

Studies of some Rural Communities in Nigeria that experienced Climate Change Impacts

These studies were carried out by some NGOs in Nigeria to discover the level of awareness of these communities about climate change impacts.

1)   The first study was carried out by an NGO called CARUDEP in two communities in Plateau State known as Dashe in Vwang Local Government Area and Kwaikong in Langtang Local Government Area with population of approximately 5000 people respectively. The study revealed that variability in rainfall is affecting the timing of planting and the length of the growing season. The people grow diversity of crops such as maize, rice, soya beans, sesame seed and groundnut.

Problem: The water table is now further down and surface water bodies like dams, ponds, and streams and rivers have been significantly diminished. When these sources of water dry up, people especially women travel between 2-4km in search of water. Lack of water has caused local deforestation because the people have resorted to selling firewood in exchange for water. The lack of water has forced schools to close down and caused water related diseases such a typhoid fever, cholera and diarrhea to increase. High temperatures have caused heat related stress leading to increase diseases in man and livestock. High temperature have also resulted to low crop yields.

Farmers in Kwaikong area have experienced years of lost of high percentage of yam seedlings due to intense heat and unpredicted rains. Women farmers have seen a decline in their harvest of guinea corn inthe past 5 years, now only harvesting 20 ties in contrast to 100 ties they produced in the past years.

2)   The second study was carried out in September 2009 by Coastal Life Initiative (COLIN) an NGO based in Calabar, Cross River State. The study was in two communities of Esuk Idebe and Akwa Esuk Eyamba, each with a population of 2000, located in Akpabuyo LGA in Cross River State. Both communities are rural settlements where fishing and agriculture are their main activities. Cross River State Coastal Zone is characterized by a large expanse of mangrove, which is importantas buffers to the direct impactfrom storms and associated erosion from severe weather, as well as providing habitat for diverse aquatic species.

Problems: Mangroves are threatened by overuse sea level rise and by the invasive species and Nipa Palm which has taken over much of the coastline in Cross River State.

Fishers in these communities are reporting low fish stocks, often returning empty handed after a day of fishing. The loss of key livelihood means that coastal communities are e vulnerable to additional stresses that may be caused by current climate change impacts such as sea level rise and possible salt water intrusion into farmlands. The communities are also facing a reduction in crop yield due to the unpredictability of rains during the growing season. These changes in livelihoods are causing about 60%of men and youth in the area to leave the communities in search of other means of income, leaving the remaining women and children burdened with additional labour.

In order to help these communities to adapt to the climate change impacts, the NGO's - CARUDEP and COLINS took some positive steps like:

In Dashe community boreholes which were broken and unusable have been restored. In Kwaikong, the dam reservoir was deepened in order to supplement dry season water supply. COLINS introduced fuel efficient wood stove to households in order to reduce labour loads and to conserve mangrove.

Results and Discussion

There were big threats of climate change impacts in socio-economic development, agriculture and health and the observation showed that the people in the rural communities and those in coastal zones of the nation are more, vulnerable. The result of the participant observation showed that the communities are experiencing incessant variability's in weather intensive heat from the sun, sea level rise, low harvest (refer to the problems) but are ignorance of the cause. The institutional framework set up to respond to the observed climate change impacts lack the capability in terms of knowledge and technological expertise. This makes sustainable development still illusive. The discovery made is that attainment of sustainable development by Nigeria is possible through the integration of HRM in the administration of the institutional framework. It has been discovered that climate change impacts have become a global problem and have received international attention but the rate of solution to climate change impacts in developing countries is low because of incapacitation by lack of technology, appropriate knowledge resulting to weak institution and weak labour force in the area of science and technology. The theory of SHRM explained that the need for inter-disciplinary approach is inevitable in terms of research and development, since response to climate change is a multi-sectoral responsibility that needs well seasoned and well trained personnel to handle.

Summary and Conclusion

Climate change impacts are drawing concern from both national and international system. The most worrisome aspect of it is its threats to all countries especially developing countries being vulnerable. Nigeria like her other African counterparts in pursuits of climate change adaptation, mitigation emergency and management by establishing institutional framework as a response to the challenge to climate change impacts have not been able to achieve success in the implementation of the policy objectives of environmental protection and sustainability as part of attention against climate impact. Some reasons adduced for the failure include lack of technical skill, corruption, lack of political will, lack of funds etc. it is the view of this paper that these problems persist because human resources management approach has not occupied the central position in the public sector administration.

Recommendations

1. The governments should adopt and support the practical methods NGOs

are using in adaptation and mitigation of climate change impacts.
2. Governments should invest fund into research and development and the private sector should support the government in sponsoring research and development in order to develop human capacity of the nation.
3. Encourage researchers to design their research to meet the societal needs.
4. Encourage multi-disciplinary research
5. Inculcate science culture in all levels of education-primary, secondary, tertiary and university.

References

Anam, B. (2012). *The Framework of Public Administration.* Calabar: Kings View Publishing House.

Arua, J. & Duru, E. J. C. (2010). *Development Administration in Nigeria, Issues, Principles and Strategies,* Abia: Nigeria Global Prints Ltd.

Aso Bur: The case for Human Resources Development and utilization Policy for Nigeria in Ali D. Yahaya and Caleb I. Akinyele (eds) *Humans Resources Development and Utilization: Policies and Issues. Proceedings of the conference on Human resources Development and Utilization Policy*, Badagry: Administrative Staff College of Nigeria (1992:53).

Beer, M. Spector, B., Lawrence, P., Mills, D. & Walton, R. (1984). *A Conceptual View of Human Resources Management in Managing Human Aspects.* New York: Free Press.

BNRCC (2007). A Report of the BNRCC study carried out in rural communities in Nigeria.

Building Nigeria's response to climate change/NEST (2012). Nigeria: Marbek resource Consultant Ltd.

CBN (2002) in Arua and Duru (2010), *Development Administration in Nigeria. Issues, Principles and Strategies*, Aba: Nigeria Global Prints Ltd.

Climate Frontline: African Communities Adopting To Survive (2009). Norway: Prinfo Unique Larvik.

James, G. Adegoke, J. Saba, E., Nwilo P. and Akinyede, J. 2010. Satellite based Assessment of the Extent and changes in the Mangrove Ecosystem of the Niger Delta. Marine Geodesy 30(3) pp 29-267.

Ibe, A. C. 2010. Capacity Building for climate change Management in Africa. In Proceedings of Working Group 11, Joint UNESCO - 10C - GOOS-AFRICA - IHP/AARSE/GEO Pan African workshop on Decision Making support for Coastal Zone Management, Water Resources and

Climate Change in Africa Cotonou, Benin, 15-17 February, 2010.

Ibe, C. M. (2010). Public education and Awareness Strategies for Managing Global change in Afica. In: Proceedings of Work.

Ibe A. C. and Ibe C. M. (2010). Global Climate Change: Myth or Reality? In: Proceedings of the UNESCO/DTCAIAU/ECOWAS Parliamentarians Quadrapartite Consultative Workshop on Climate Change and Policy and Legislation, Accra, Ghana, 20-21 October, 2010. Abuja: DTCA pp. 16-29.

Ibe, A. C. and Ojo, S. O. 1994. Implications of expected Climate Changes in the Coastal and Marine Environment in West and Central Africa. UNEP PSRS NO. 148 (In French and English).

IPCC for Policy Makers (2007). In Climate Frontline: African Communities adopting to survive (2009). Norway: Prinfo Unique Larvik.

National Emergency Management Agency (NEMA). National Capacity Assessment Reports. Part (1), June 2012, Draft Vol. 3, Federal Republic of Nigeria.

Nwosu, A. F. (2012). Managerial Problems in Human Resources Management (HRM). A discovery from Forestry Commission, Cross River State, Calabar (Unpublished seminar paper presentation in Political Science Department, University of Calabar).

Oba, U. B. (2005). "The Impact of Human Resources Administration on National Development: The Nigeria Experience in Contemporary issues in Public Administration (ed) Duru, E. J. C., Ikejiani-Clark M. and Mbat, D. O. (2005) Anambra, Nigeria: Mojo/CYMART Ventures.

OKeke, P. (2002). A layman's guide for Privataliation, daily Champion, 24.

Stolper, W. (1966). Planning without facts: Lesson in resource allocation from Nigeria's Development. Cambridge, Massachusetts: Harvard University Press.

Storey, J. (2001). Introduction: From Personnel Management to Human resource Management: A Critical Tex, London: Thomson Learning.

Uwadiegwu, B. O. and Muoghalu, L. N. (2012). Addressing the challenges of Urban renewal through Citizen Participation: Lesson from coal camp renewal project in Enugu City, Nigeria (Seminar paper accepted for Publication).

WDI 2000-2003 Qtd in Arua and Duru (2010).

Wikipedia, Free Encyclopedia.

World Development report: Development and Climate Change (2010).

Washington DC: The International Bank for reconstruction and Development and the World Bank.

World Development Report: Development and Climate Change (2010), Washington DC: The International Bank for reconstruction and Development and the World Bank.

Ibe, A. C. 2011. Towards a low carbon Economy: A National Climate change policy for Nigeria. A policy Document prepared under contract for the special climate change unit, federal ministry of Environment, Abuja. ACI

Environment and resources Nigeria Limited P27.

James, G. Adegoke, J. Saba, E., Nwilo P. and Akinyede, J. (2010). Satellite Based Assessment of the Extent and changes in the mangrove ecosystem of the Niger Delta. Marine Geodesy 30 (3) pp 29-267.

Ibe, A. C. (2010). Capacity Building for Climate Change management in Africa. In Proceedings of Working group 11, Joint UNESCO-10C-GOOS-

AFRICA-IHP/AARSE/GEO Pan African Workshop on Decision making

support for coastal zone management, water resources and climate change in Africa Cotonou, Benin, 15-17 February, 2010.

Ibe, C. M. (2010). Public Education and awareness Strategies for managing Global change in Africa. In: Proceedings of Work.

www.ingramcontent.com/pod-product-compliance
Lightning Source LLC
Chambersburg PA
CBHW020414290526
45785CB00002B/551